Innerscape

Robert L. Schwenck

Edited by Lorna Collins

Cover Design: Larry K. Collins

ISBN: 1537421301

ISBN-13: 978-1537421308

ASIN: B01LBTOQOE

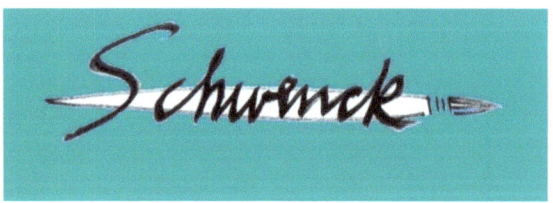

http://www.schwenckart.com
schwenckart@cox.net

This version contains a Foreword by Allen D. Koehn, D.Min.; L.M.F.T and several additional images.

Who looks outside dreams

Who looks inside awakens

~Carl Jung~

CONTENTS

FOREWORD

When we first see these paintings with their vibrant colors and diverse powerful images, we are likely to question their meaning and messages. Knowing how to name or define something provides one way to process new information and expand your understanding.

The artist provides detailed written descriptions of each of his challenging and inspiring visual works. These are a wonderful resource and I encourage you to take the time to read them. Words and pictures each have a distinctive power of their own.

That said, I urge you more strongly to delay reading the words and first give time and attention to each painting and establish your own immediate, intuitive and spiritual relationship with the images. Perhaps go ahead and smile at the playfulness, open to your reactions to the images, and scratch your head at the possible incongruence of figures and actions portrayed. Your personal courage in approaching the delights and demands of these multi-leveled works will create a unique relationship that will then be enriched when you add Bob's words to your own experience. Enjoy.

Allen D. Koehn, D.Min.; L.M.F.T.; Certified Jungian Analyst; Professor Emeritus Pacifica Graduate Institute

DEDICATION

This book is dedicated to the memory of

Erin Lynne Schwenck

1968 – 2010

The daughter we always wanted and the mother of three of our grandsons

ACKNOWLEDGEMENTS
WITH THANKFULNESS

Lorna Collins   - for her persistence and her editorial and computer skills

Larry Collins   - for his photographic skills.

John Sanford   (now deceased) - for walking with me through some very deep water in counseling

Bernie Schwenck - for always being by my side and supporting me even when she has not understood

PAINTINGS AND WORDS

The paintings are primary. They came first. They are not illustrations of my words. The paintings emerged before the critical thought. They arose from my inner world before I wrote any words about them. These paintings emerged from my soul and my murky unconscious. The mixture of images—angelic, human, animal, architectural or botanical—is intuitive. They were not painted in any logical storytelling sequence. They contain some consistent references like the memorial arch at the Presbyterian Church in San Juan Capistrano dedicated to our deceased daughter, Erin. The church and gallery facades are actual places where experiences important in my life have been a blessing. All these images are used poetically, without the demands of historical logic.

I hesitated to publish my comments because usually the artist is the least qualified to interpret his own work. The viewer's unique response is much more significant than the artist's. Yet I dare to write about what cannot be contained in words or in the paintings themselves. I hope these paintings and the words accompanying them will help others see their lives, their struggles, their successes, their failures, their faith, their doubts, and their pain and frustrations from a more balanced and hopeful place.

The unseen world of spirit is real and active. The world of bodily, dusty life is more obvious and often seem more important to us. Questions abound because of these realities. How do we understand their interplay? How deeply does each penetrate the other? How do these paintings relate to them? And how does the artistic endeavor relate to it all? When everything is painted and all is written, I still do not have the answers to these questions. However, scripture speaks to these questions, and our inner life is at work to reveal some of the answers. I hope these paintings will help.

The theme of time is important throughout these paintings. The time we are allotted for this evolving life is limited. This reality feels like a threat to some. To those who have faith in a Divine Presence, the journey becomes less threatening and a more an exciting adventure. For those without faith, death is a dark end to be avoided, even in thought.

The images of the clock and the hourglass encourage us to value each moment with their present joys. While we are unable to firmly grasp the deeper truths and their mysteries, the creative artist can point to them and offer an invitation to peer into the dark. I hope this insight will lead us to a place of humility and thanksgiving for this wondrous, awesome experience of life.

And so we paint, we write, we sculpt, we sing, we act and dance, even though we remain perplexed.

Robert L. Schwenck

Artist

2016

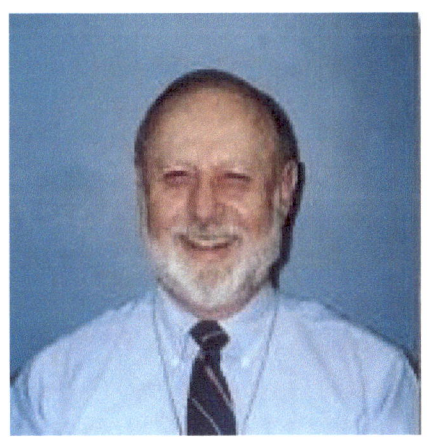

THE YOUNG MAN AND THE LAMB

(40x30 oil on canvas and 11x14 oil on canvas)

The young man smiles. Life is full and promising. Gently he holds the soft lamb. The lamb is calm, reassured and trusting. Is he protecting the animal? Or is it protecting him? The young man hopes for a day to come when the lamb and the lion will lie down together. He dreams of the time when the child and serpent and ox will not be threatened, when war is no more, and hatred, anger or fear are not forcing sacrifice.

An angel with pink wings and flaming red hair descends to the beautiful young man to embrace him and reassure him in his dreaming. His holding of the lamb is approved. To hold on to creative, wondering innocence is a blessed thing. To make sure it has a meadow to be nurtured in and quiet waters to be satisfied by is a holy way to be. Even when the lamb is to be slain and its blood spilled to the ground, the good heart and the believing soul hold on to the beauty of the lamb. The meadow will be there. The cool waters will flow and peace within the violent cosmos will come.

A golden young woman glides silently upwards toward the full moon and passes through the young man's mind. She is beautiful, illusive, magical, very desirable, but a little out of reach. The mountain and the ocean wait for the sun to rise as the golden female soars even higher. The whole earth anticipates the fullness of the sun to appear and bathe the land in light. Vision and consciousness are coming.

The eager young man holds tight to the lamb. He will sing a song of creation, a song of deep time. The angel encourages him to sing. "Sing to the Mother. Sing to the Spirit. The Shepherd of the earth is present."

8

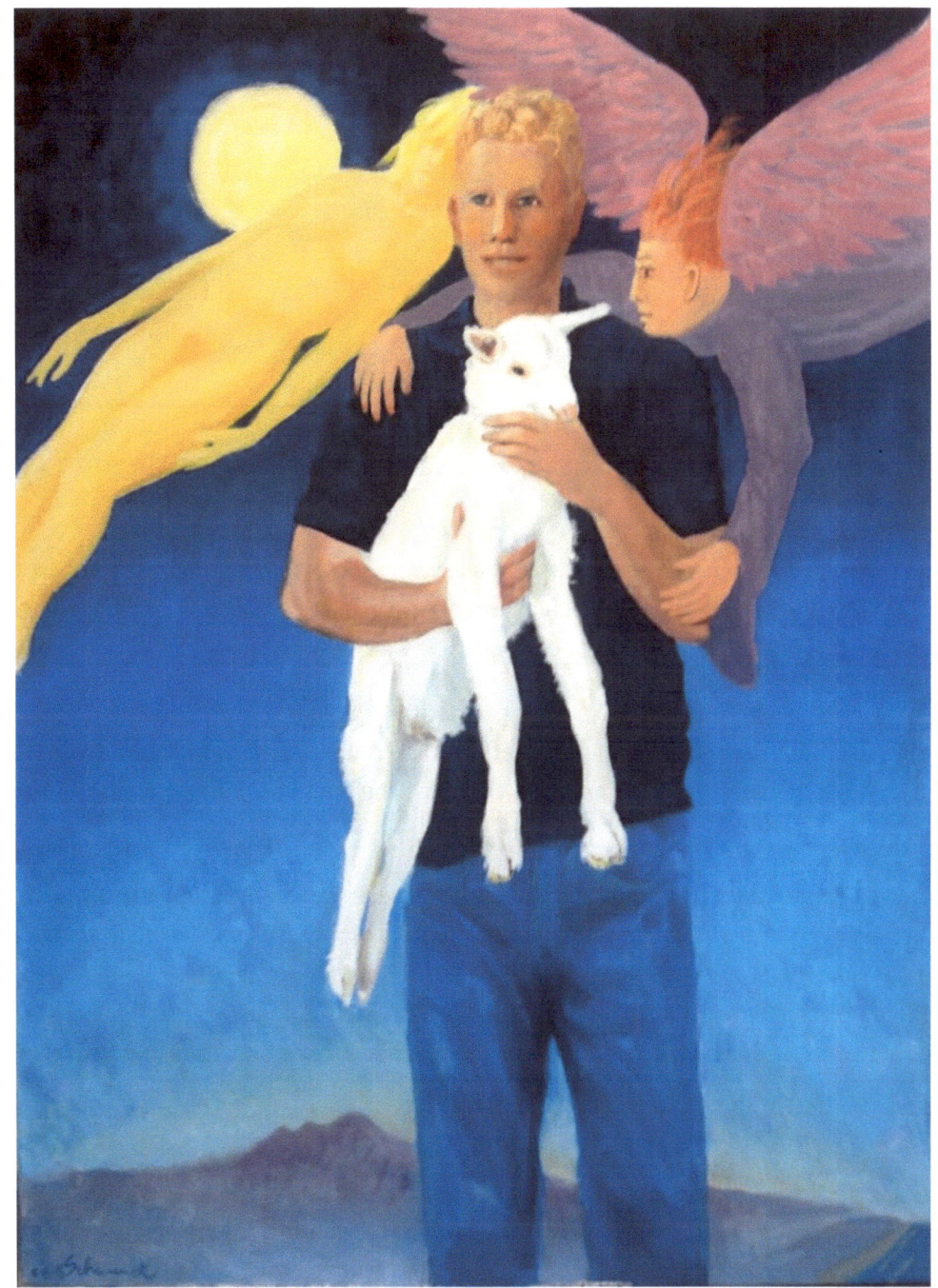

A BALANCING ACT

(40x30 oil on canvas)

The life of every human is a balancing act between the clown on the right hand and the beast on the left. The clown, trying to be profound, is funny to some and frightening to others. He is offering the sacraments as he leans over the beast. He is part of the religious effort to communicate the divine. He is so sincere, yet so unable to portray his faith fully.

In a dynamic tension with the ministering clown is the wild beast. The brute has the face of a man, and with his powerful energy, which rises up from his animal nature. He offers the instruments of creativity. It is a holy equilibrium. The balanced soul sings out, 'Holy, Holy, Holy," and dances for joy. He is bathed in a golden light. His joy flows from within the difficult balance of the clown and the beast.

A passionate energy comes from above, an angelic horsepower. The archangel points to the creative balance. It is heaven-blessed. Balancing the equal and opposing forces of clown and beast is the Creator-given engine for all life and art.

 The angelic horsepower brings with it the knowledge that this dynamic life is time-sensitive. Life has an end. The sand in the winged hourglass is trickling away. Yet this disturbing insight has light in it because every hour is pregnant with life. It is a cosmic gift. This time-gift is there for the one who will courageously balance the clown and the beast.

Nearer to the viewer's awareness is the bouquet of joyous experiences and the sweet tastes of life's goodness. Every vivid soul needs to share a creative response to the depth of life. Thus, the gallery, or the book, or the pulpit, or the stage. Like the hourglass, the memorial arch is a reminder of death's reality. The bull's movement through the arch is irresistible, passionate, and dangerous. The bullish finality of earthly life steps forward into the mature consciousness, and each moment, every vivid experience, every relationship becomes precious.

The green watcher looks up at all this lively activity and sees the need for balance. What he also sees is a flock of seven golden swallows flying through passion into the light. The watcher is filled with wonder, awe and thankfulness. Then he picks up the brushes, palate, and canvas and begins again.

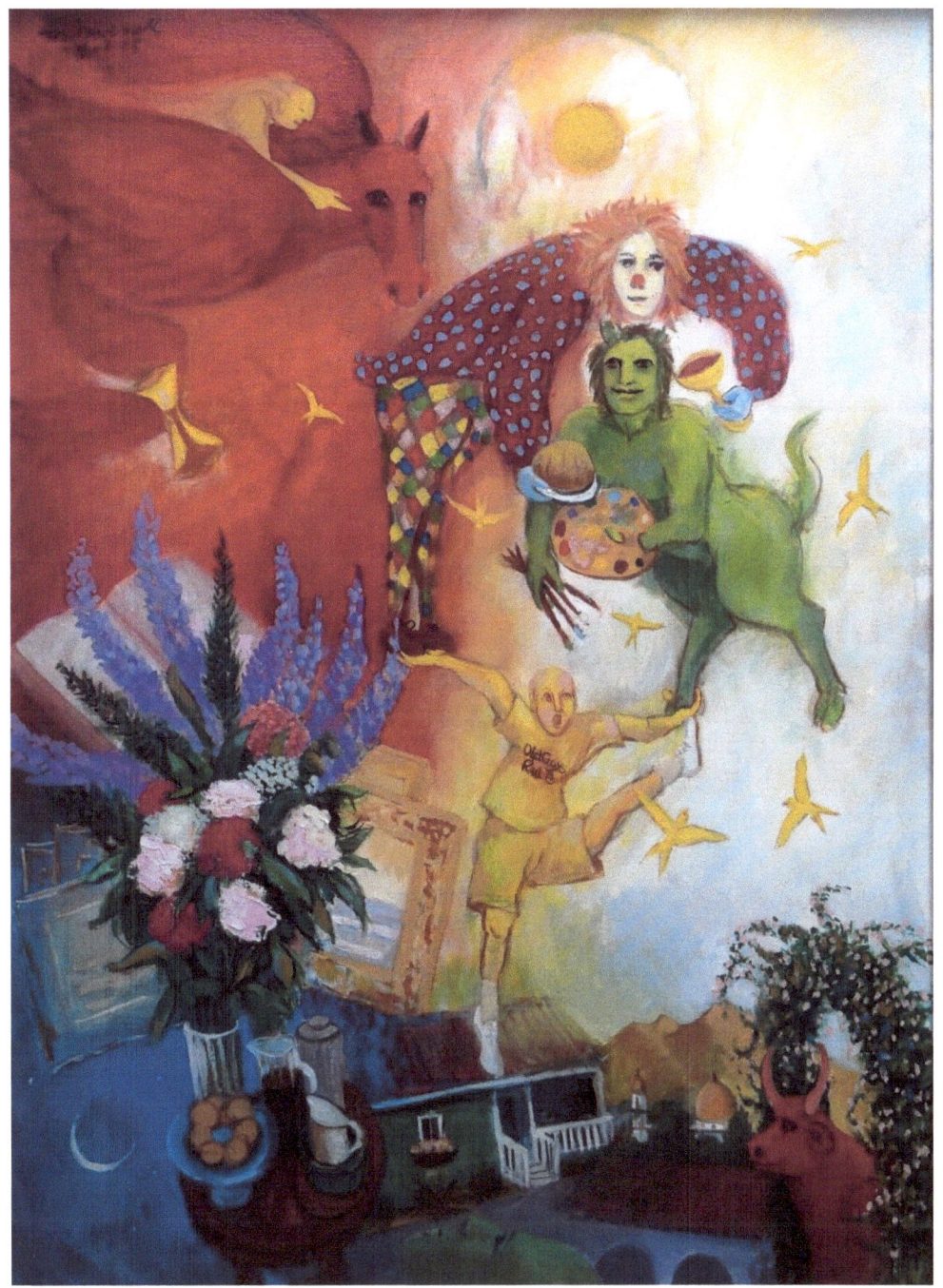

NIGHT RIDER

(30x40 oil on canvas)

The artist stands by a moonlit sea and peers into the vast sky. Overhead, the feminine spirit rides a wild horse. She is unclothed, vulnerable, and she clings to the horse's mane desperate to stay on. Her red hair flows back. She stares ahead, determined, always moving forward through the night. She never stops, never rests, never retreats, never retraces where she has been. She is chased by an angelic power, which holds a glowing hourglass. Time is short for her ride through the dark. Each night, each moment of powerful insight in every soul's dim consciousness moves too fast to understand it all. The artist looks up to see her gallop by, anxious to record everything, but it is not possible. The creative effort is much too slow and inaccurate to capture the vision, which speeds by above the moon and the glistening sea where leviathan lives unseen with all the other mysteries of the psychic world.

All the creative person can do is salute the muse, wave to her, and then put a few strokes on the canvas. The painting is not in view, for it is only a pale gesture and not the reality to which it points. Creative work is inherently frustrating and often depressing because the artist, writer, preacher, or actor can only wave with appreciation at the vision, but never capture it whole or even alive. A painting is too shallow. Writing is too approximate. A poem is too vague, and the theatrical too self-conscious, the relationship too incomplete. The human's creative work is but a gesture, a hint of the fleeting insight and intuitive feeling, which holds eternity in it. The insight and feeling gallop by, and we are left with only a hint. We stand frustrated, longing, and inadequate. No matter how prepared we are, no matter how many tools or brushes we hold or colors we've mixed, or time spent with the beloved, they are inadequate to express even a small bit of the depth we have felt and seen. No words, images, sermons, or gestures can adequately express what we experience fleetingly and understand vaguely. Yet, creators are impelled to try to express their visions. They are prodded and pushed by their own souls to create. Is it cruel? Is it a blessing? The answer is yes. It is both.

Two lovers embrace. In their naked passion, they experience the mystery of spirit. They soar over the dark depths where monsters abide. In the climax, they experience the flesh becoming spirit and spirit becoming flesh. In that overpowering moment, the veil between flesh and spirit thins to a spiritually permeable membrane. The angles of God fly to the moon to celebrate. There is joy in heaven. Bright blooms are offered when the nightrider passes by. Something eternal is present. Three red-winged black birds peer out at the human scene, blood on their shoulders, hunger in their guts, waiting to fulfill their journey when the sun rises.

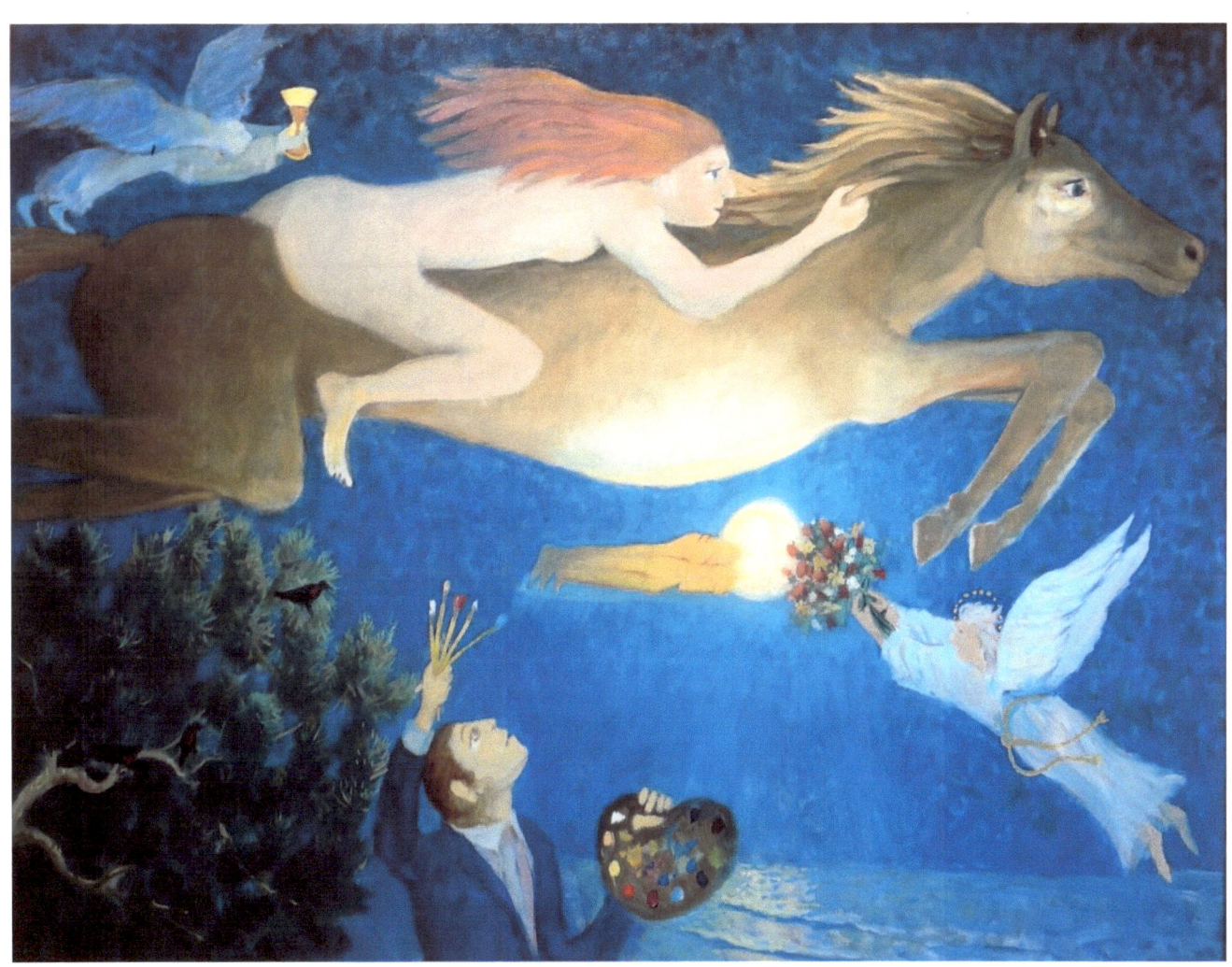

SUNRISE LOVERS

(30x36 oil on canvas)

Mature lovers embrace and declare their love for one another again. They are clothed. Passion and urgency have aged and mellowed to become gentle support, reassurance, affirmation, and a listening ear. They are lifted above the mundane and the beast below on the back of a white dove. It coos a soft, soothing melody for them, "The beloved is here. The beloved has no fear." They are relaxed and comforted.

As they fly onward, the sunrise expands. They renew their marriage vows. A new chapter in their long marriage begins. Although the dove carries an hourglass, running low, they still have time to grow and experience each other in new ways. Awareness expands as the vivid sunrise pushes away the night. It is time to see life more clearly. A star, which has guided the lovers, remains for a while, and the sliver moon begins to fade. Day is coming. Clarity will dawn.

The dove carries paint brushes. These are tools with which to describe the beauty and warmth of life. The palate for mixing colors descends with a green angel in a pink flowing gown. He comes from the highest heaven and trumpets the news: growth and creativity are possible. The means for further growth are at hand. With these good gifts, the angel also brings the fruit of Eden, the knowledge of good and evil, consciousness and thus responsibility.

Creative powers can be good or evil, blessing or curse, shallow or deep, selfish or offered freely. The lovers' relationship will help to keep the power of creativity in focus as they give themselves into each other's arms. Good choices will be made. Joy and thankfulness will be expressed and shared. They will be a blessing to others.

Below the soaring couple, the dark, primal beast waits and watches to see what will be done between the wings of the dove, what choices will be made, what authentic expression will take place and what soul work will be accomplished. The beast knows their time is slipping away. The day will not last forever. He knows what goes up must come down. Life is grounded in the earth. The dove cannot fly forever. It will tire and descend to an earthly reality both frail and temporal. The expanding day will fade into another night. But for now, the promise of the rising sun and other sunrises to come blesses the lovers. Appreciation and thankfulness for what they have been given wells up in their hearts. For now, the lovers soar above the powerful beast and the dark sea.

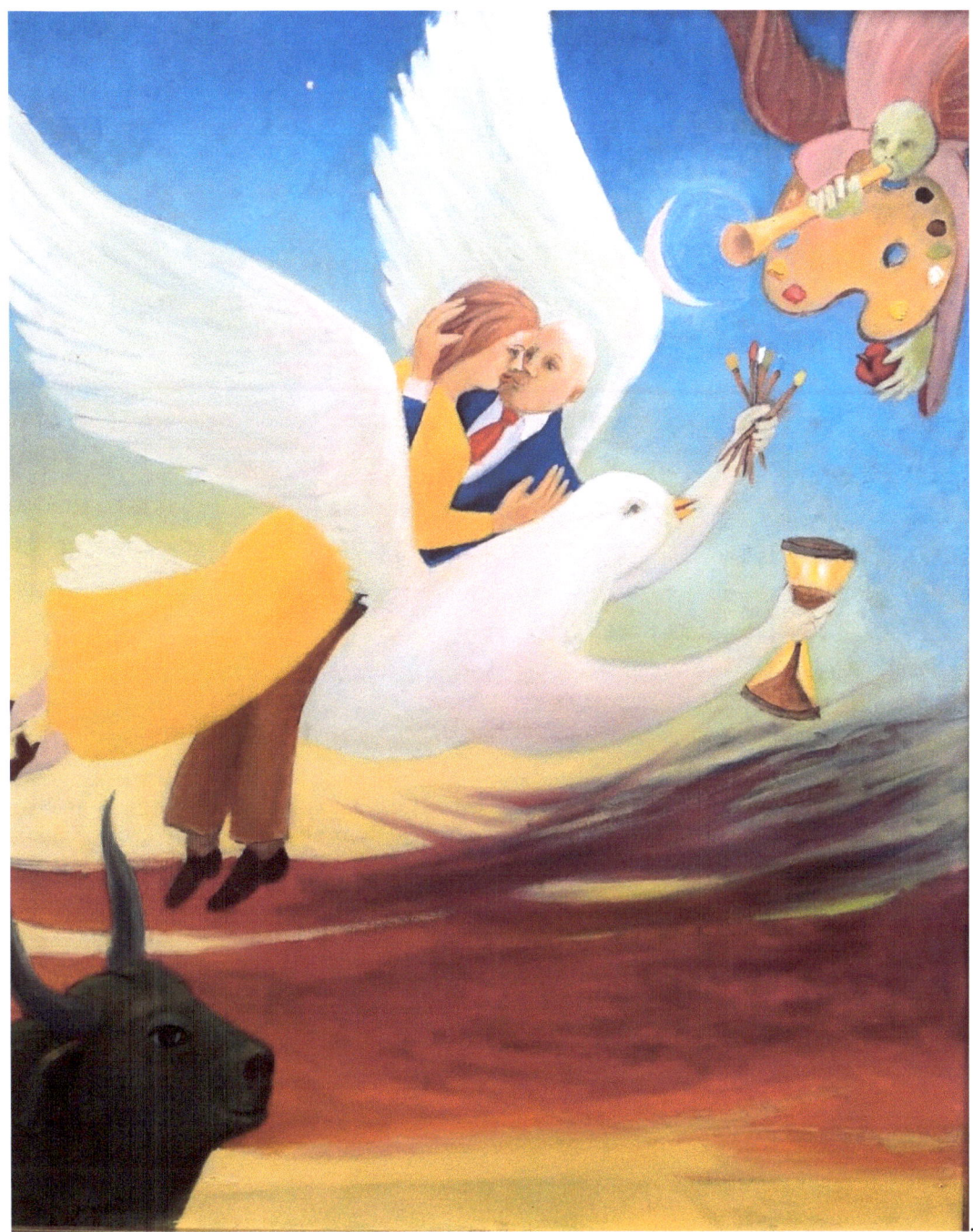

RAINBOW RIDE

(24x20 oil on canvas)

A gentle spirit flies to bring light to lovers. The soft-winged spirit smiles as it illumines the love they share. Light shines softly on their naked bodies and reveals the husband's creative passion. He is aggressive and eager. She is warm and receptive. Over their heads, she holds a vase of blooming yellow roses. He holds his artist's brushes ready to paint.

They ride the leaping rainbow high into the night sky. The rainbow cannot stay aloft for long. It will fall back into the deep waters from which it came. How will the lovers fare? The artist has painted the rainbow and incorporated the yellow bouquet. Three angels support the canvas in process and celebrate the love it portrays. Heaven blesses the earth. The earth brings pleasure to the heavenly realms.

All this happens in the dark of a starry night. Within the unconscious, only a little natural light from the small slice of the new moon permeates. It shines on the surface of the deep, calm sea where leviathan lives and illuminates the pink roses on the memorial arch, which rises above a bed of red roses. More light is needed before the rainbow's strength fades.

Thank God for the light from the red candle in the hand of the gentle spirit. Thank the Creator for bodily passion and creative commitment between lovers. Thank God for those leaping, soaring moments and for rainbow experiences. Thank the Lord of heaven who blesses the earth and all that is in it. Amen.

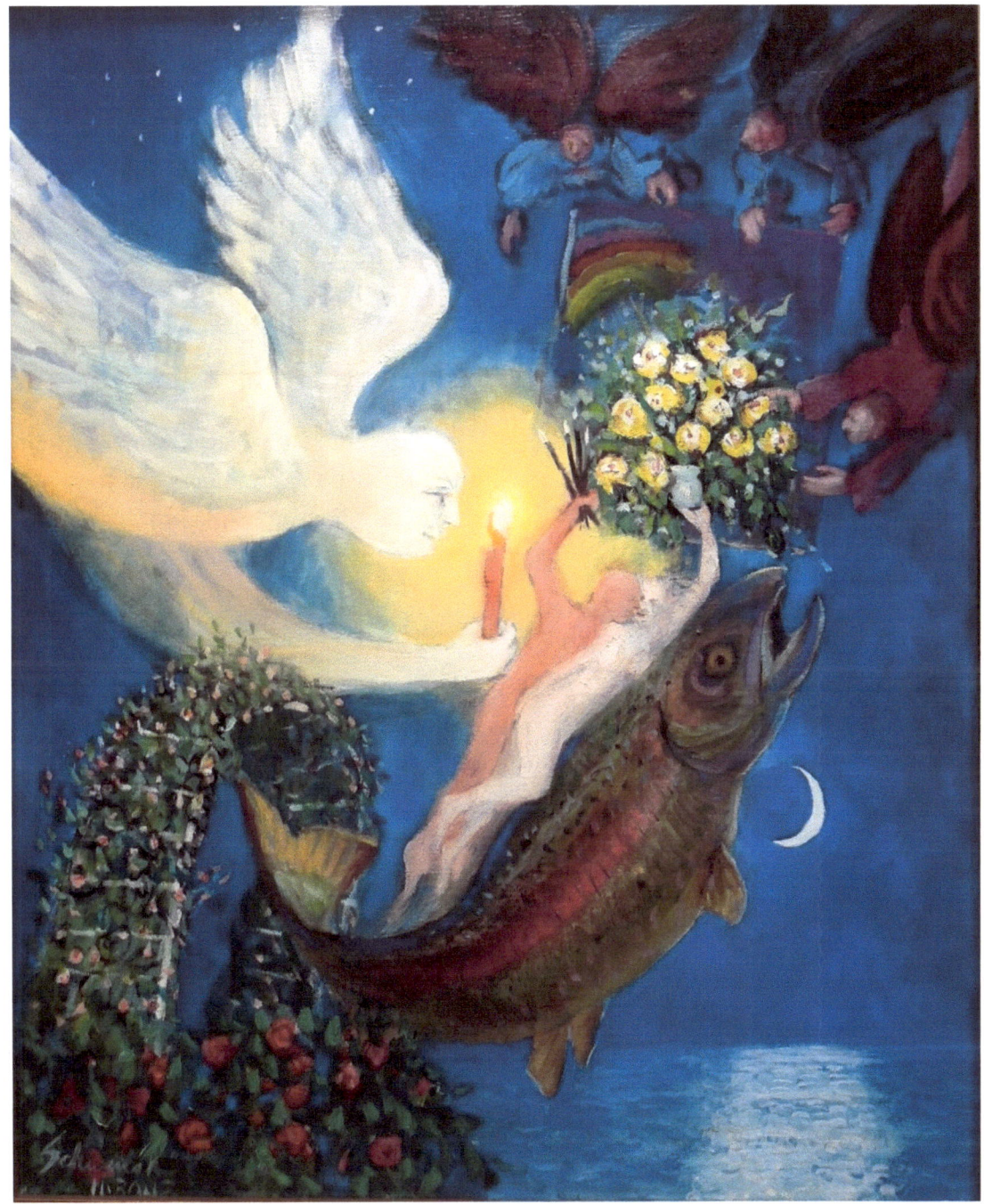

IT'S ABOUT TIME

(40x30 oil on canvas)

The new moon has the fruit of Eden hanging in its center. The enticing fruit is part of our universe. New light is becoming brighter, and it always brings a great temptation. Each insight is not the whole truth nor the complete picture. The great serpent, the spokesperson from God's garden, passes by the source of the knowledge of good and evil. It comes from heaven to earth, from the unknown dark into the light of earth. It is God-sent. It comes from mysterious eternity into the limitations of place and space, the home of flesh and blood. The serpent flicks its searching tongue at the pendulum clock and smiles. It thinks it knows the truth. All things change, all things die.

Each moment arrives like an irresistible locomotive, like a huge wave. It cannot be stopped from arriving. It cannot be suspended in place. The moment moves into and through our awareness and then is gone, leaving room for the next powerful moment. Time moves through the memorial arch from light to dark and tells us life in the body is short and limited. Death is real. The awareness of this perishable moment of time shines light on the church and its beliefs. They are changing. The mountains stand tall, and yet they are evolving. Eternal truth stands strong as the Creator is revealed, not evolving but revealing. It is our understanding which evolves.

The Creator Spirit brings time to us. It is a gift, though brief. Within the Spirit, who gifts us with time, is a desire for communion, where the temporal communes with the eternal. The bread and the cup speak of this. The church has the privilege of sharing it with the world. All bodies are broken. All life is spilled out. Death is real, but it is not the end.

From the unknown depths, the rainbow leaps into consciousness and carries multicolored time with it. It is beautiful, vital, and powerful, but it can stay airborne and be seen for only a moment before its creative glory falls back into the depths. This vision is a gift.

Whatever authentic talent, skill, training, or opportunity we possess is in service to both time and eternity, flesh and spirit. Artists reach out through their colorful palettes, and with brushes, seek to describe what they know of the fleeting vision and the glimmering beauty. The effort is a sweet taste of nectar for the fragile spirit. The man in the blue blazer releases his spirit for creative work where the blooms of earth are near the memorial arch. Time, change, and death are always with us. They are irresistible. But for now, we have the gifts of beautiful blooms and sweet tastes and fragrant scents in the star-studded cosmos.

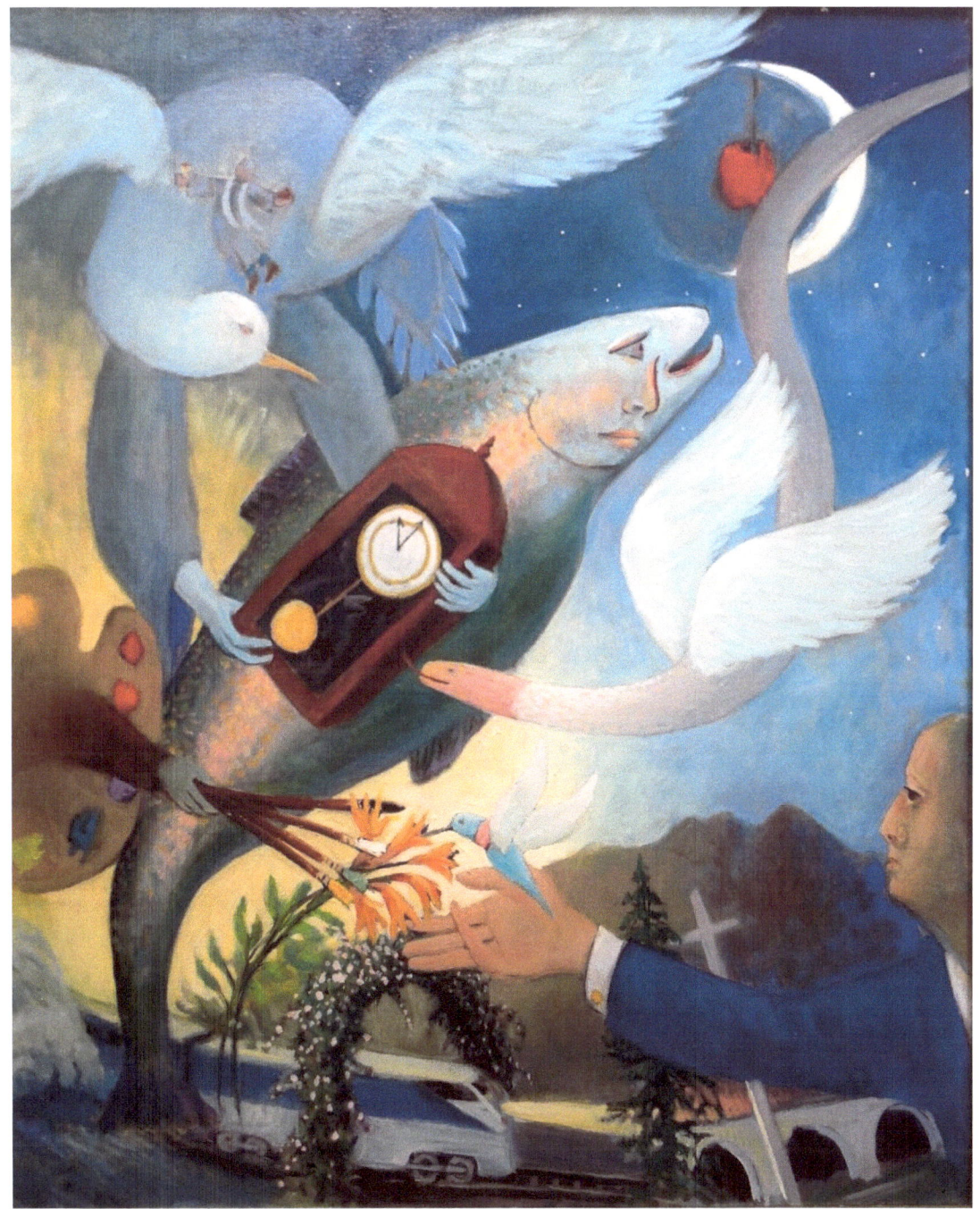

FULL MOON

(36x30 oil on canvas)

The full moon derives all its light from another source. It cannot emit its own light from within. It is beautiful but dim. The human condition, always in subdued light, is derived from another more intense primary source reflected in nature, love, and creative arts. Moonlight reveals much about the world within and around us to the awakened consciousness. An angelic presence comes passionately with flaming hair, offering the cup of communion. With it, she brings the uncomfortable knowledge of the finiteness of time. Our limited vision peers into a dark mystery, and we are dumfounded by our mortality.

There is much sweetness to taste in this life. Like the hummingbird, we flit from one beautiful bloom of goodness to another, and we sip gratefully of the nectar of lover, children, grandchildren, long-time friends, and the animal life which teems all around us. The young woman rides on passion. It is powerful, dangerous, creative, and thrilling. The young woman sits astride aggressive, primitive instincts, on the horns of a dilemma. Tension leads to the fullness of life. It stretches human logic between extremes, and leads to insights, creativity, sweetness, and joy. This awareness stands in front of the memorial arch, dedicated to a loved one. It opens to a deep darkness and mystery, which the light of the full moon cannot penetrate.

The important physical places on our journey mark discoveries, moments of insight and courage. The stability of the mountain, the history of the Mission, the gallery, and the present space to exhibit creations are steppingstones on the journey. The power of the Creator aligns them as a pathway. The successes and failures, the joys and grief, the logical and the confusing all play an important role on our journeys. They become a beautiful bouquet of fragrant life, blooming at our feet.

For those who become aware, who begin to see, even though dimly, life is a wild and wonderful ride. Like the surfer who glides on the energy of the wave, we ride the swell of instinct and exciting discovery in relationships, in art, in commerce. We do not make the wave. We do not generate the swell. But we, with skill and daring, go gratefully with its flow, seeing in the light of the moon the gifts of communion and time. The light we live by is dim and secondary. Those of traditional faith acknowledge how small a light they have been able to offer others. Yet it is light, small though it may be. There is no room for hubris. When we shine humbly, the full moon becomes the harvest moon, full of promise and adventure, even though all around us is the mysterious, unknowable darkness. Yet we move on.

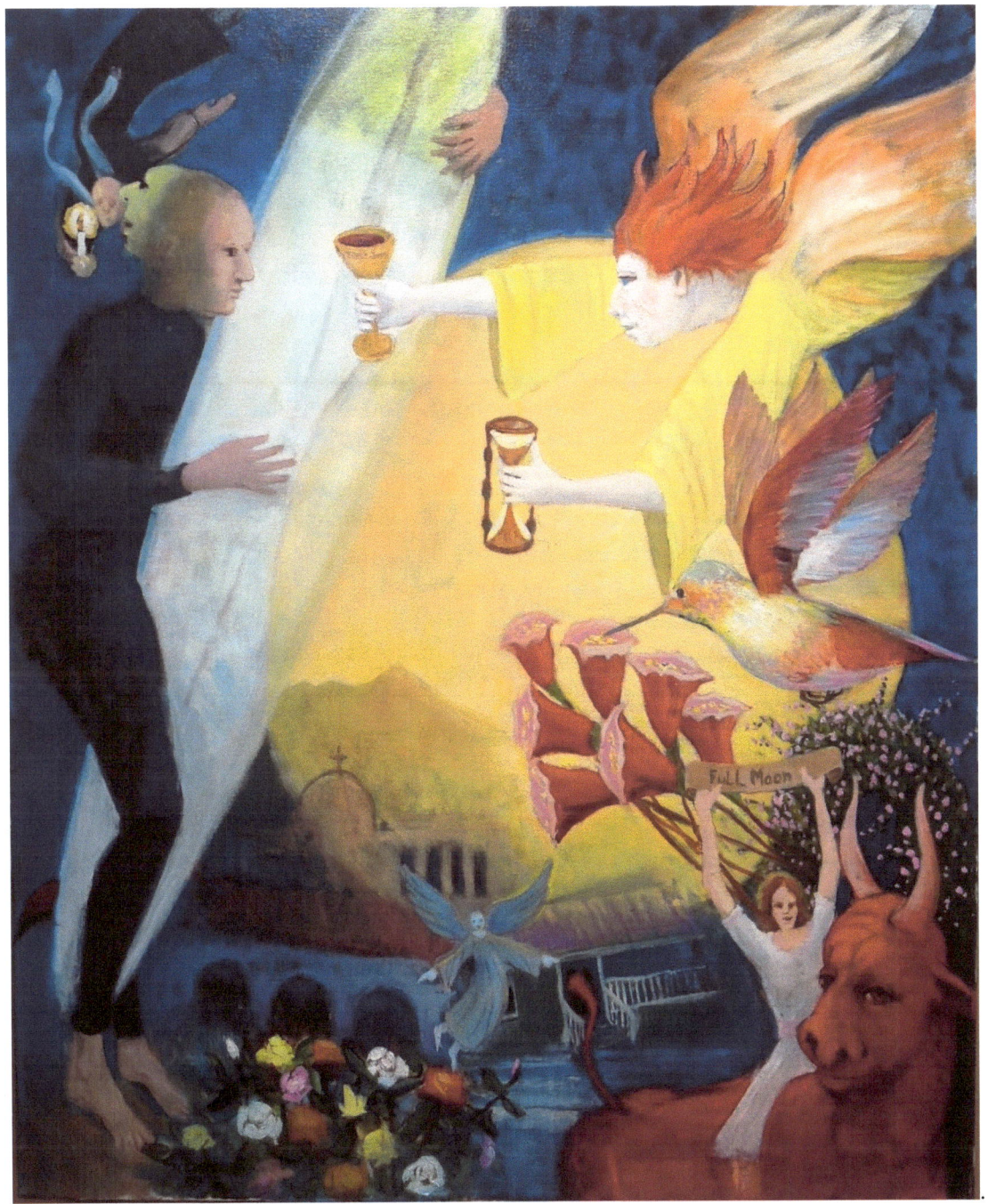

THE PREGNANT WOMAN

(36x30 oil on canvas)

The whole universe is with child, pregnant with life. All stars, the moon, the sun, and all spiritual beings are anxious to see what shall come forth from the womb of the universe. The woman, dressed in white, is holy. A nimbus glows around her head. Her hand moves to her swollen belly and feels life stirring. She smiles and is deeply satisfied with the implications of her fruitfulness. She reaches out to touch the serpent. It slides in and out of the whole cosmos. From the stars, through the Spirit, past the man and woman, it winds. It is colored in stripes of fleshly pink and vegetative green.

The tempter's voice comes from deep in the garden created by God. "You will be like a god and know the value of all things, whether good or evil. You will be a law unto yourselves." New ideas come to the woman and the man. "To know more is a call to grow, to understand, to take control, to be responsible, to create, to become more conscious, more whole souls, to know about good and evil." The green man reaches out to her and draws her toward him. He is on the edge, almost out of the picture. He offers the power to seed, to grow, to bloom. She will incubate, nurture, and expel new life from her holy womb. They need each other.

Behind the man and woman, the great blue Spirit is supreme among the stars, the moon, the sun, and beyond into the heart of the universe. The Spirit smiles as his great blood-red wings surround the man and woman. Suffering is at the core of the universe. The Creator shows his wounded hands. The Spirit knows the pain soon to grip the woman as she squeezes life out into the cosmos. He will suffer with her. His smile will broaden.

The dark green messenger of the Creator brings the winged hourglass into the world. It glows with energy and vitality as time slips away. Time flies. The memorial arch floats upside down in the middle of the Spirit-filled environment. All our expectations about death and loss are reversed. Death, which seemed so huge, is actually small. What seemed devoid of blossoms now flowers brightly. What appeared empty has life flying all around it. What seemed solidly embedded in life actually is uprooted. Death has no firm foundation in the cosmos. Death is overwhelmed by Spirit.

The whole universe is pregnant with life. The seven golden swallows swoop around the memorial arch. They sing a song of joy and celebration. "Life is good and full of grace. All creation is full of His glory." The life-pain is starting. The birth is close. Feel the movement in the belly, touch the serpent, taste the fruit, absorb the knowledge of good and evil. The contractions have begun. The whole cosmos is ready to birth more life.

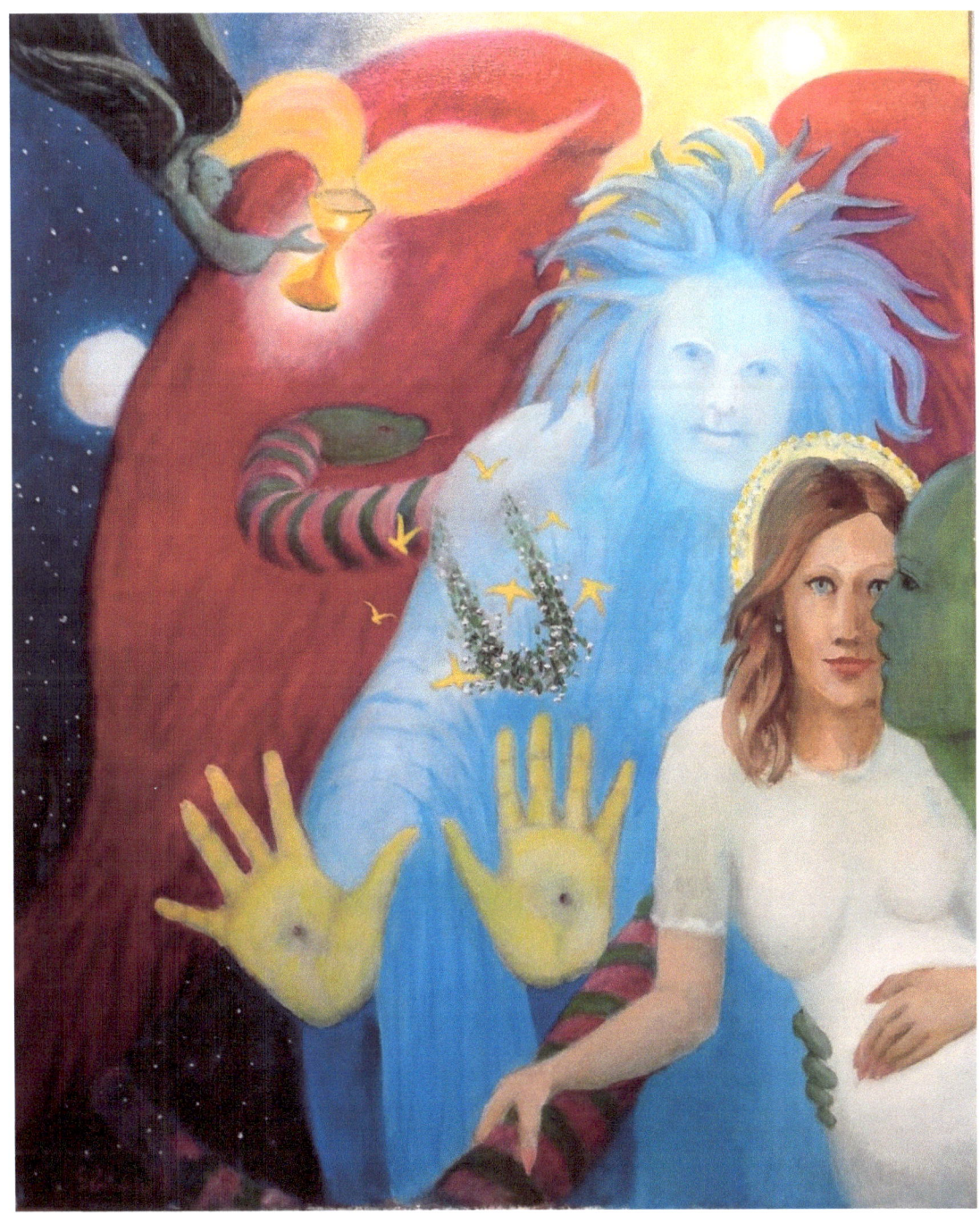

THE GIFT OF TIME

(36x30 oil on canvas)

A golden angel soars on great wings of passion into the presence of the lovers. In her hands, she brings the glowing hourglass. Time is set in motion. Life evolves. Each moment is a gift, running out, but filled with light, full of wonderful possibilities. Time is limited. To know time is finite for each soul is a source of wisdom, insight, and knowledge. This awareness is frightening to some and often buried in a dark place. Regardless of resistance, time flows on, and all changes and evolving it brings in the environment, body, mind, and relationships cannot be halted.

The passionate man and woman embrace on the back of the great red bull, their powerful animal-instinct. They rise with the bull into the light. Their passion will slip away through the hourglass. Night will come, and time will be no more.

The green man represents a source of growth and expansion. He offers a gift of beautiful, scented blooms to celebrate her beauty and the sensual pleasures they give to one another. She is earthy with flaming red hair. Fire is in her womb. From God's Eden, she brings to the relationship the fruit of consciousness and the knowledge of good and evil. The man is a creative source. She is incubative, warm, full of life.

Life is a good gift.

During the night, the spirit figure swoops from the other side of the blooming memorial arch into the presence of the lovers. They hear the spirit sing, "Alleluia, Alleluia, Gracious is the Creator and sacred is the gift of life. Alleluia." Life and time are blessed. Life comes from life. The passionate animal seeks the sun and carries the lovers with it. They, too, sing the hymn of praise, "Holy, Holy, Holy is the Lord of heaven and earth, the giver of all good gifts."

The elements of Christ's communion come into the light, borne by the pastor. He swings on an unstable trapeze anchored in heaven. He wears the white stole, the yoke of Christ, and smiles broadly. He is joyful, privileged to share the body and the blood of Christ with all who see in the bread and wine the very presence of the Creator. He sings, "Alleluia, Alleluia. Gracious is the Creator and sacred is the gift of life. Alleluia"

And all the people say, "Amen."

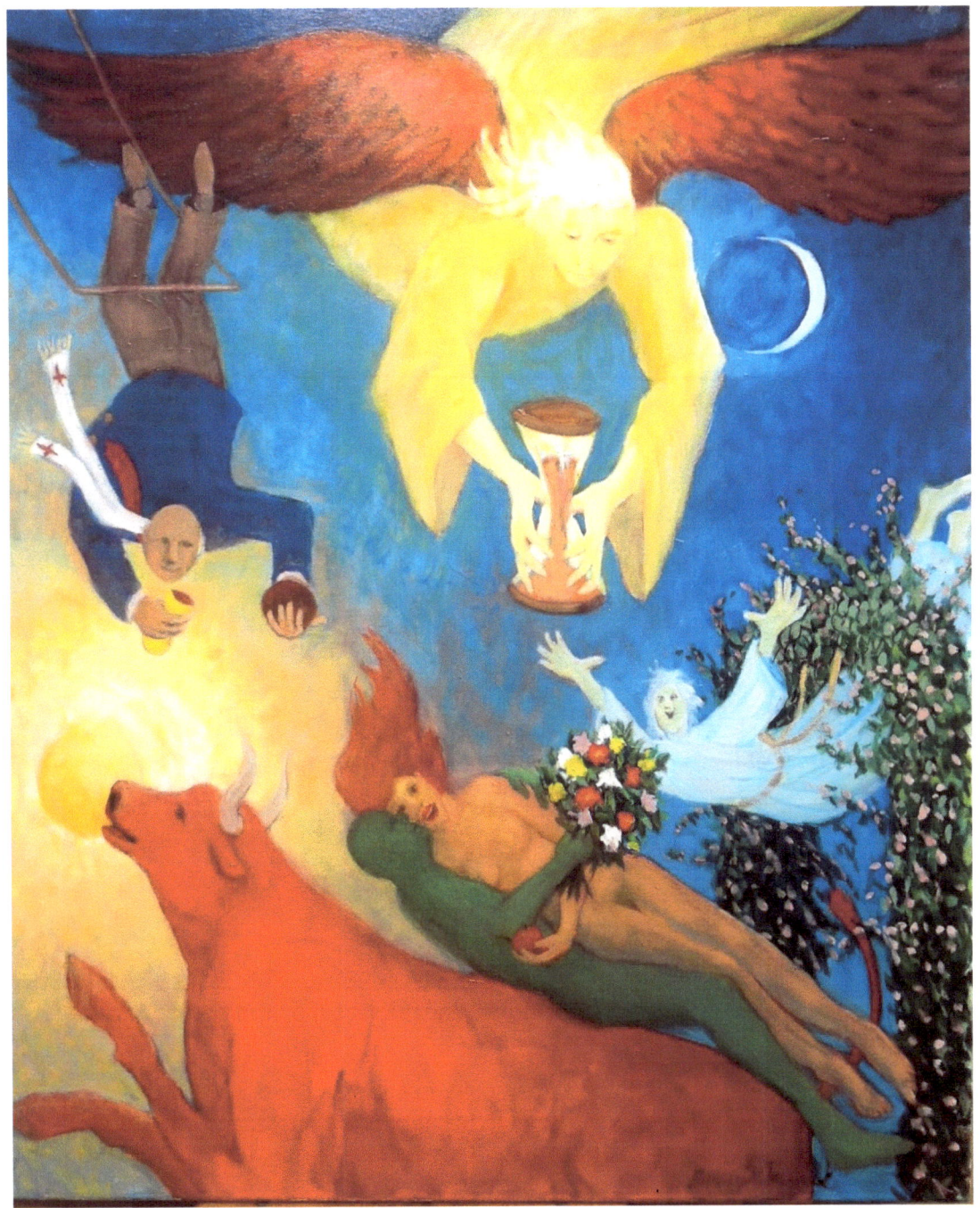

THE HERO AND THE BEAST

(36x30 oil on canvas)

The beast emerges through the memorial arch, from death into life, from darkness into the light. The brutal animal is huge and full of primal power. It moves slowly through the arch, dedicated to a deceased child. The arch is covered with blossoms of pink roses. The horned beast looks back. It will return to the other side, but not now. It is not evil. It is a dangerous power from the dark. The beast is smiling. It means no ultimate harm, although its horns are sharp and deadly. Its brute force can trample the strongest of us. The presence of the beast has caused the arch to bloom with beauty and abundance.

Why is the beast present now at this difficult time? What does it intend to do while it is present? Why does it allow the amputee to stand on its back? Many questions remain unanswered. For now, it is simply a powerful support for the maimed man. He has had his right leg amputated above the knee. Yet, he is able to stand on his left foot without his crutches. His balance is miraculous and solid. He raises one crutch like a javelin. Is it meant for the beast? Will he try to kill it? Subdue it? He is wise enough to know he knows he would be ineffective against the primal force, which comes from death into life. The one-legged man looks to the scriptures made present by angelic power and sees the smile of the beast as real. It can be counted on.

The maimed man is dressed half as an American hero and half as a jester and clown. Perhaps he is a war hero or perhaps he represents all people who have experienced life's difficulties and traumas. Life can maim physically, mentally, emotionally, and spiritually. He has crutches, but he would prefer to stand on his own. His courage is great. His determination is strong. A heart is embroidered on his chest, a reminder of the vulnerability at his core. Is his heart weak, in danger of giving out? For now, the center of his life sustains his body and soul. Thank God for his heart.

The golden angel blows his horn announcing the hero's courage and bold exploits. It is heaven-sent music. It is music not heard by everyone, and unwelcome noise for many. Those who are heroes, who limp and struggle with vulnerable hearts, can hear it clearly. The hero sees a sliver of moon in the darkness. The scripture is brought to him by an angel dressed in pink and soaring on red wings. The hero turns to see. He is encouraged. The moon gives off a faint light by which to read. The moon rays glisten off the vast sea and remind him of how huge and awesome the visible and unseen worlds are. In the depths of the sea, great mysteries dwell. Leviathan lives there. The hero is safe on the back of the beast.

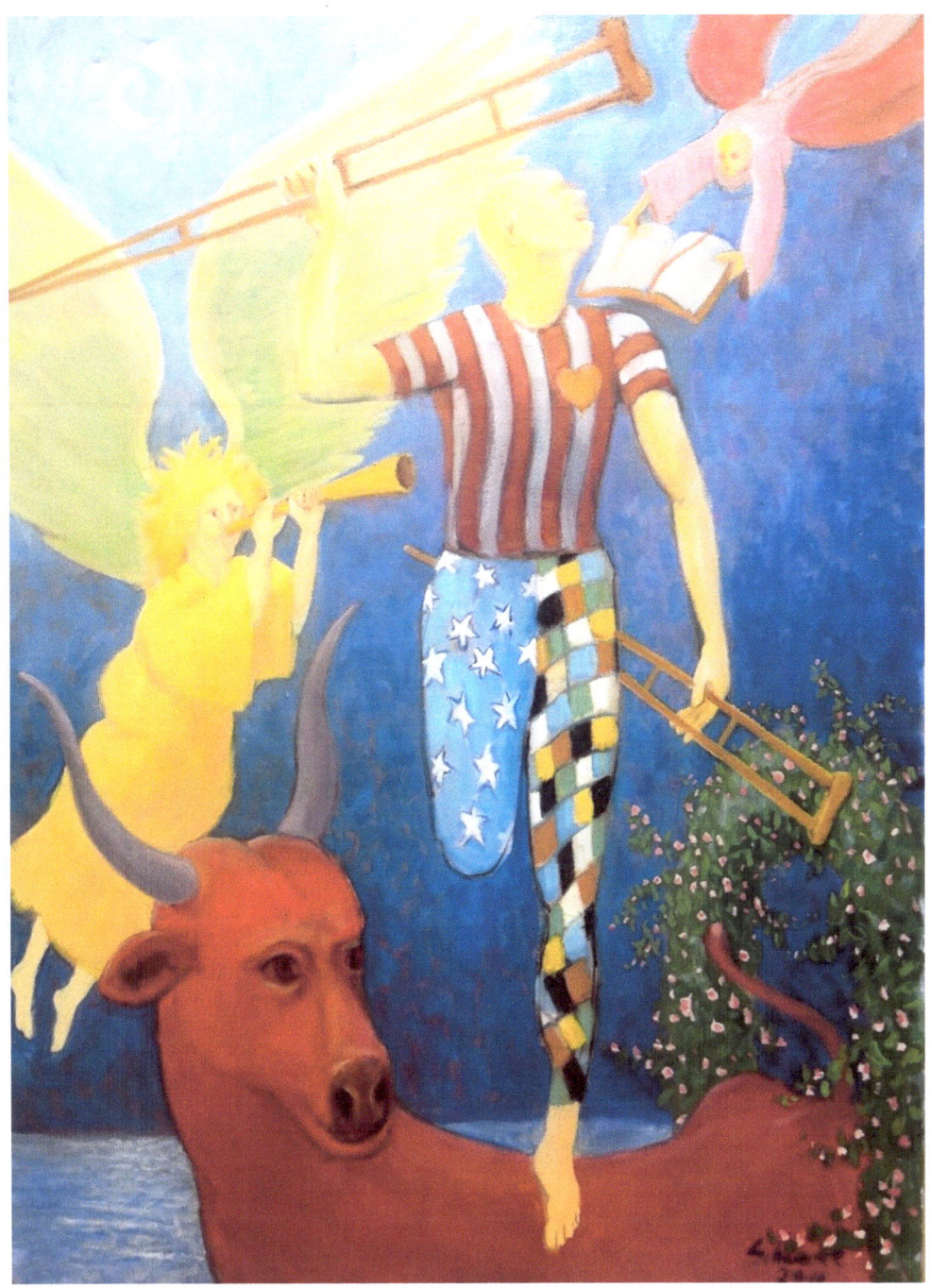

THE SWINGERS

(36x30 oil on canvas)

The clergy person, gowned in green, brings a bouquet for his beloved. He swings across the landscape, heavy with the tradition of the church and held up by his wife. His work depends on the strong grip of the feminine. She hangs precariously from a trapeze with one leg. It is the best she can do. The trapeze is anchored in heaven. What it is attached to is not known. The connections to the spiritual realm are not clear. The couple is just thankful the anchor holds strong. Life is tenuous as it oscillates back and forth in a wide arc between the light and the dark.

She is dressed in white. Her blonde hair flies around her head like a halo. She swings in a golden light and is determined to hang on. Their relationship and his work depend on her strength and commitment. He swings toward a night full of stars and a thin moon that gives off only a little light. Together they fly above the church, the mountain, the deep sea. Waves pound the rocky shore. The persistent surf surges through the memorial arch. The source of life floods forward. The pendulum clock rises out of the mysterious waters. It counts the minutes, the hours, and the days. Life moves swiftly on. Time surges forward leaving less and less opportunity to swing together or do the work of ministry. Life is short.

The hummingbird hovers among the red blooms and tastes the sweet nectar. The flowers swing through the arch. Awareness of mortality heightens the sweetness of each blossom. Every day is intoxicating. The winged ones sip, taste, and drink deeply from the earth's pleasures. Life is good.

Above the swingers, an archangel points out the broken bread and poured-out wine. The Creator's self-giving is without limits. The pastor's message is clear. Nourishment from divine sacrifice is for all peoples everywhere. The minister celebrates this eternal grace even though he is in precarious circumstances. Life is dangerous.

Below, the watcher takes all this in. He wonders. He questions. He knows he must be patient, watching in the dark. All is not clear. Time races on. Strength inevitably wanes. Blooms begin to fade. Grip begins to weaken. The pastor and wife hear the pendulum swing. The clock's second hand ticks, and finally the chimes ring out. For now, the couple swings above it. Life is exhilarating.

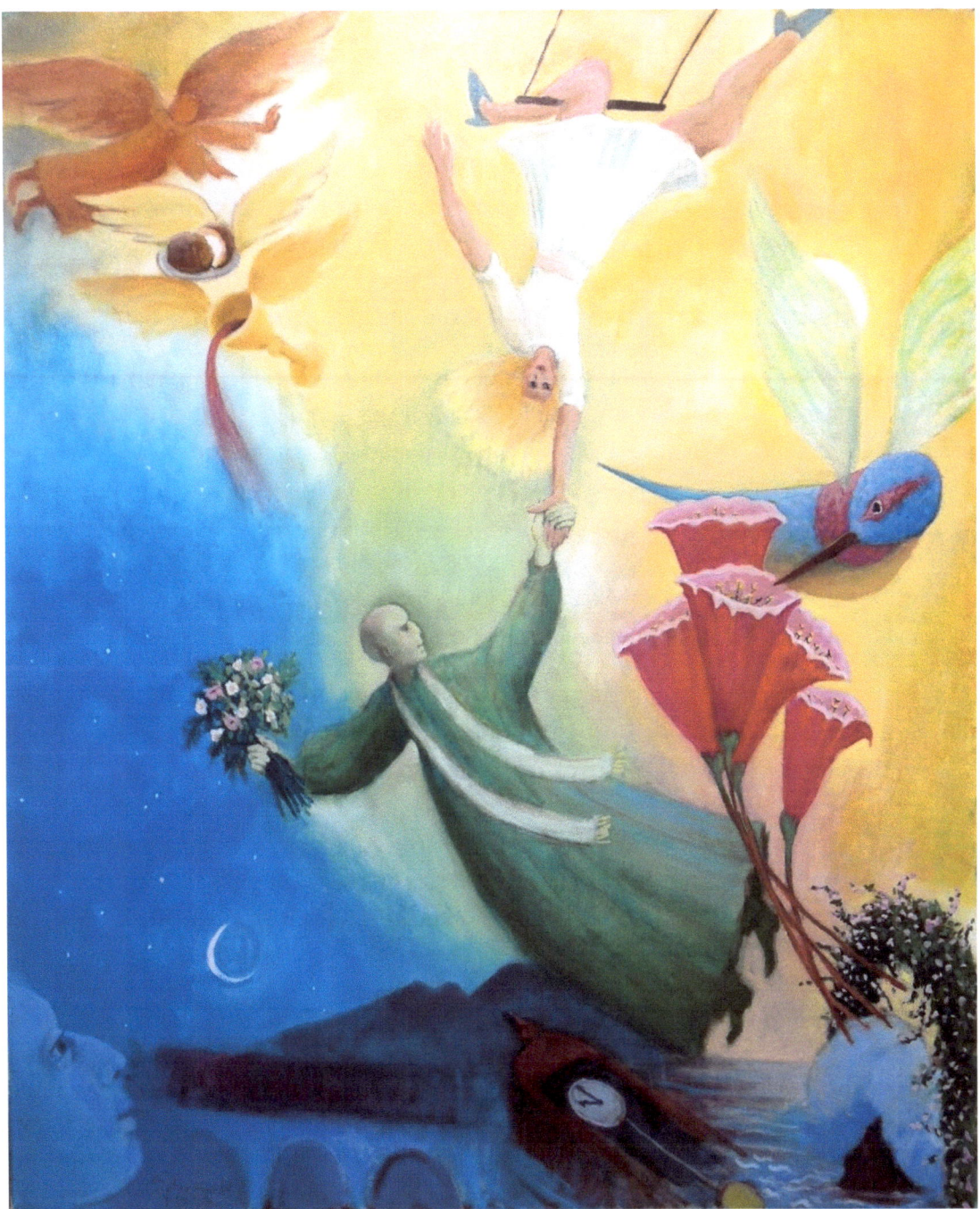

TRADITIONAL FAITH

(36x30 oil on canvas)

A life of traditional faith lives in a specific place and time. It is not separate from the dusty path walked daily by those who believe. It is also lived out within the vastness of the cosmos. The temporal exists within the eternal, and faith believes the eternal lives within the created order. Faith partakes of a specific time and place as well as the timeless and eternal. This-world experience is like a filter, which colors the eternal, perhaps even distorts it. However, it is the only way to access the part of the truth we are capable of grasping where we are.

The Christ figure hovers over the couple on wings of passion. Passion brings him forward into our world. His green face speaks of our growing understanding of the spiritual power so near to us. Spiritual life is never static. It is always evolving, growing, as our life changes and our experience teaches us greater truth. Great loss results when a soul seeks to stop life in place. Being aware of this process helps us to be open to the next revelation and nuance. The Christ holds out his nail-pierced hands as proof he means us no harm, but will suffer with us in order to be present with us. His suffering is not only a real historical fact, but it also reflects the character of the Creator. The source of his suffering then and now is the self-interest and egocentric attitudes of human beings and the institutions and traditions we use to protect and maintain our safety, comfort, and sense of superiority.

The traditional symbols of bread and wine, of body and blood, are sacramental and describe a real presence. The bread will be broken and consumed. The wine will be poured out, taken in, and absorbed. There is brokenness and a poured-out love from the heart of the cosmos. The aging pastor brings the communion elements to his community. He has the love of his wife to support him, the scripture to guide him, and the Spirit to empower him. The couple floats gently over Dana Point Harbor. The antique sailing ships, The Spirit of Dana Point and The Pilgrim, stand at the dock in the moonlight. These ships have sailed the vast oceans and braved great storms. They now lay quiet and still. Their journeying is done. The older pastor is ready to retire, to be docked. Yet a small skiff heads out into the moonlit deep. New adventures, new challenges await.

An angel stands on the headlands and blesses the couple. She holds a multicolored bouquet in her left hand. In her right hand, she holds artists' brushes full of color, ready to paint, a new challenge. Joy glows on the face of the angel because of the richness in their lives. Love in their marriage and adventure in the creative work are celebrated. The full moon bathes the couple in soft light and glistens on the quiet ocean where the great leviathan lives.

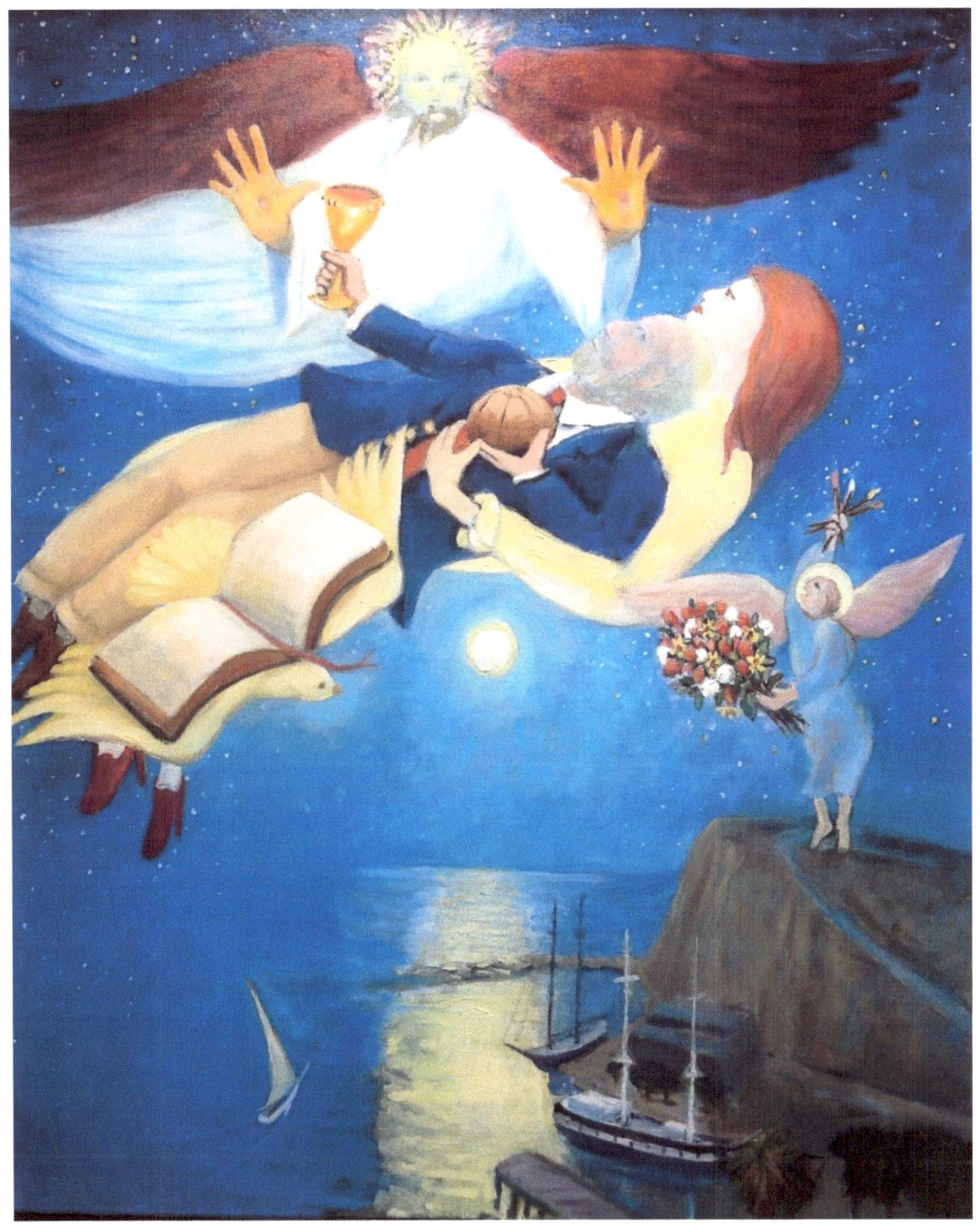

HOLY FLESH

(30x40 oil on canvas)

Earth becomes holy when it brings forth life, because the Creator is in the process. The pregnant woman is of the earth and heavy with child. She is near her due date. She is fatigued and exposed to danger, pain and the unknown. She feels the child moving within and is filled with many questions. From the shadows she worries, and is filled with doubts about the future. Yet she is surrounded by a halo of light. There is holiness in the bringing forth of new life. The birthing is announced by an angelic trumpeter descending to the woman from an all seeing Creator. What song does he play? It is a melody of new life. 'Holy, Holy, Holy, Lord God Almighty, Heaven and Earth are full of your glory." The Spirit of communion hovers over the pregnant woman. The elements of body and blood sacrificed are in his hands. Golden, heavenly wings suspend the angel dressed in white. Flesh becomes holy when it brings forth life.

The communion elements speak of sacrifice and self-giving that becomes nourishment for others. Bloody birth is a poured out cup. The broken bread calls her to offer her flesh to be split open. She will jeopardize her life for the beloved child. She is a mother of life. She is holy.

Above and in the midst, the all-seeing, all-knowing Creator shines light into the creative process. The divine presence will sacrifice in order to nourish. We will become stronger when we partake of the gift. Perhaps this is the song the trumpeter plays.

The leaping bull sails over the eye of God. Above the divine knowing, higher than it should be, the bull lifts itself with dangerous confidence. Yet there is joy. The beast glows from within. Its sharp horns are held high. Will it be a sacrifice? Will it sacrifice its animal strength for the spiritual communion in the flesh? We do not know. We are invited to enter the joy of the Creator's presence and the mystery of flesh becoming holy.

With pain and blood she will give birth and holiness will be near. Her hand feels life moving in her womb. She is in awe of the miracle. In her left hand she holds the fruit of Eden. It is a gift from the Creator's Garden. It opens the human consciousness to the knowledge of good and evil. It is the pathway that leads to becoming fully human and responsible. Even though it will lead to pain and suffering it is a holy journey. Spirit becomes flesh and flesh become spirit and from it comes life. The dangerous male animal is too high. The mother of life is too far below. In the middle the eye of God sees the angels announce and offer communion. There is singing in the heavens, "Holy, Holy, Holy, Lord God Almighty, Heaven and Earth are full of your glory."

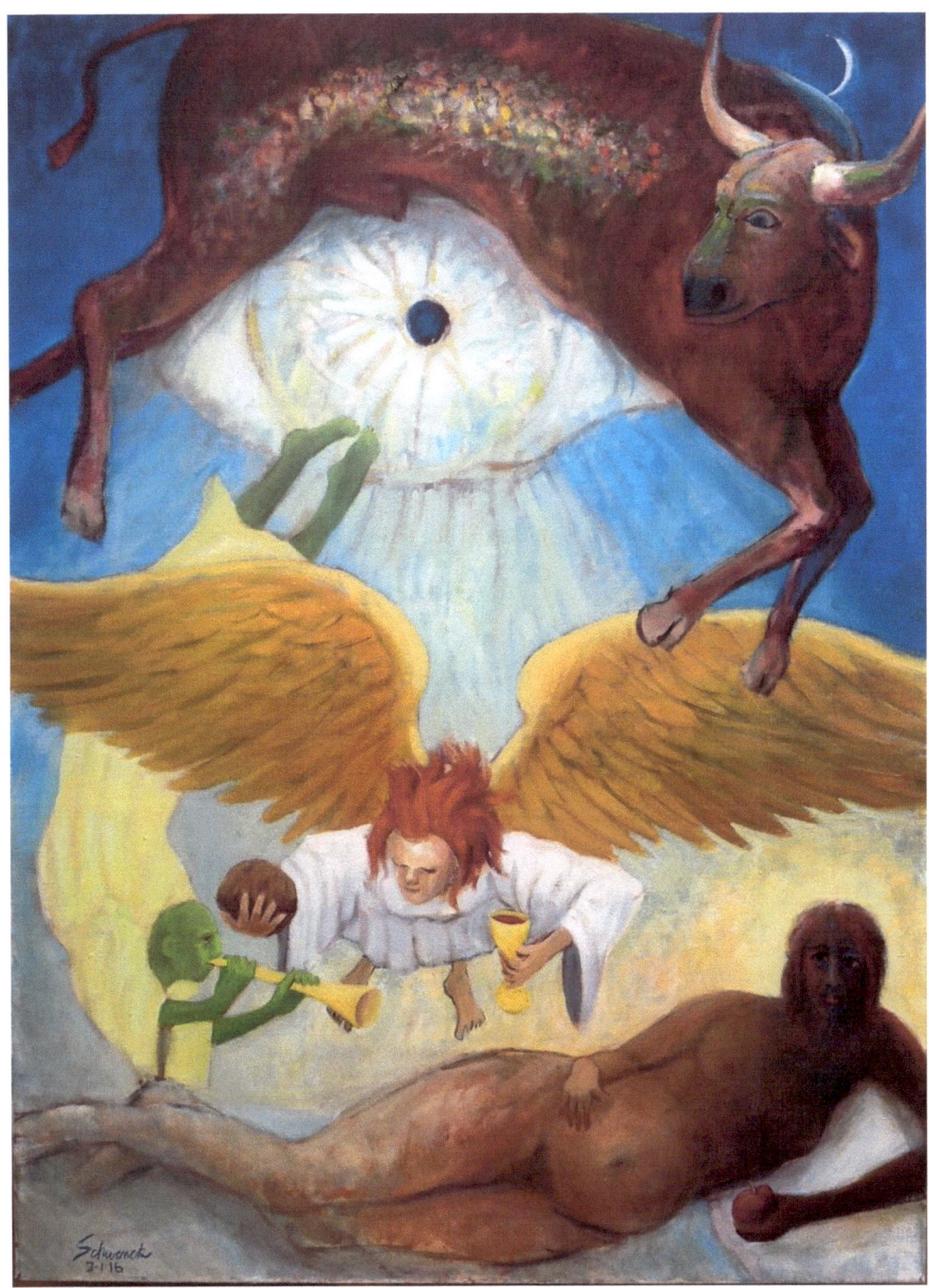

YOUTH IN BLOOM

(30x36 oil on canvas)

How fleeting is the exquisite beauty and purity of a young girl? She blooms bright and vibrant. She is full of wonder, hesitant before the mystery of her femininity. What unknowns reside in her? What will womanhood bring as her body changes? What will love with a beloved be like? What will irresistible life forces create in her and through her?

She sets astride the brute force of passion and her sexuality glows as he touches the dangerous horn. The beast is quiet for now, but soon he will be aroused. She carries a beautiful bouquet. Who has given it to her? She is waiting to find out.

An angel flies from heaven and touches her with spiritual awareness. It is not just the energy of youth, nor the passion of the flesh, nor the beauty of her bodily life coming alive. There is also a deeper awareness of her soul in the angelic embrace from the Creator.

The green brute climbs the insecure ladder to see better from above. Consciousness and insight into the wholeness of life comes when she encounters masculine power. The green brute holds the fruit of Eden, the knowledge of good and evil. Slowly, she becomes aware. Responsibility and difficult choices come with the sweet taste of taking her life into her own hands. Like a powerful train on its tracks, her development is inevitable. In the background, the church is there to help give insight, support, and encouragement. The memorial arch reminds her this wonderful pregnant moment will not last. Time speeds on. It flies away even for those who do not see it rushing away. Youth in bloom is beautiful, powerful, creative, and fleeting. Life is good.

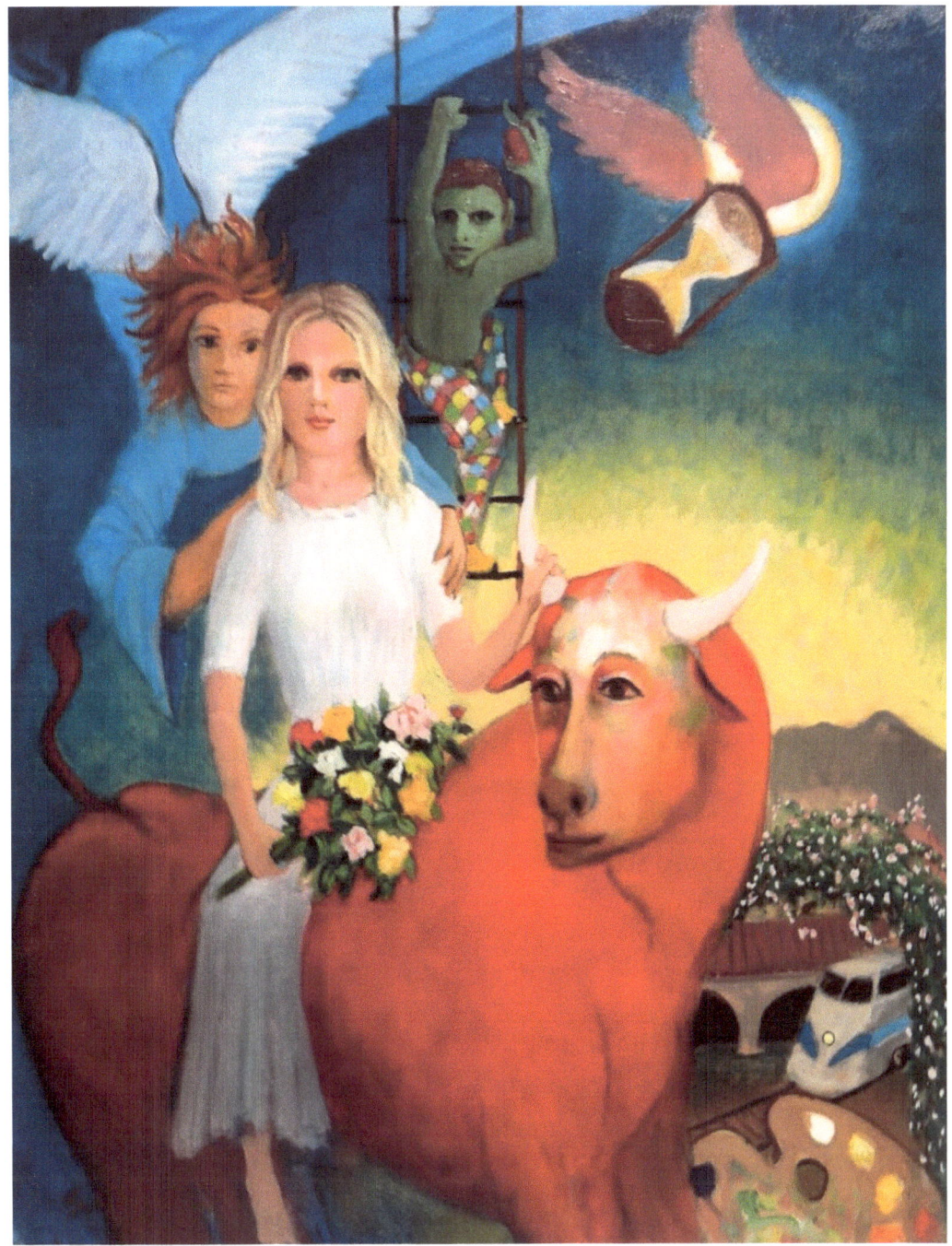

THE EYE OF GOD

(40x30 oil on canvas)

The eye of God sees all, knows all, understands all no matter how dark the night. The cosmos is not blind. The heavens see.

The night provides very little light, but there is a glimmer, enough for the artist to paint by. There is enough illumination for the beast to be seen. It is close enough for its warm breath to be felt.

The great soul sea is calm. No storms loom on the horizon. In it, the great mysteries of Jonah's depths move below. Someday they will surface and be known.

The great and powerful beast stands on the shore with its horns sharp and dangerous, but for now it seems peaceful and patient. The crucified Christ appears within the head of the beast. Will the animal be crucified? Will the animal be sacrificed?

A woman dressed in gold reaches out to the powerful animal. Does she want to push it away or does she want to touch it tenderly? Will this awesome power be part of her relationship? A man, wearing green and tan, soars over the bull. He hovers over and around the woman. He brings a light pink rose and a bold sunflower, two children, different spirits. The woman holds a bright bouquet of flowers, precious grandchildren have bloomed.

The man and woman kiss. They are very much in love. They are present for each other, each in a unique way. Angels fly around the beast. One plays a sweet melodious flute celebrating their love. The other angel blares out an announcement, "He sees, He knows, He understands. Sing glory to the Creator forevermore." They are blessed. Do they know the eye of God sees them? Do they feel the happiness of the heavenly angels? Do they understand the need for sacrifice? The night holds little light, but they feel their love for one another and are delighted with the beautiful blooms.

The artist is upside down viewing the relationships from a different angle. His hand seeks to grasp and hold the brushes dripping with color. But the brushes are beyond his grasp. They have a life of their own. The painter is ultimately not in control. Yet the artist continues to paint with energy and hope.

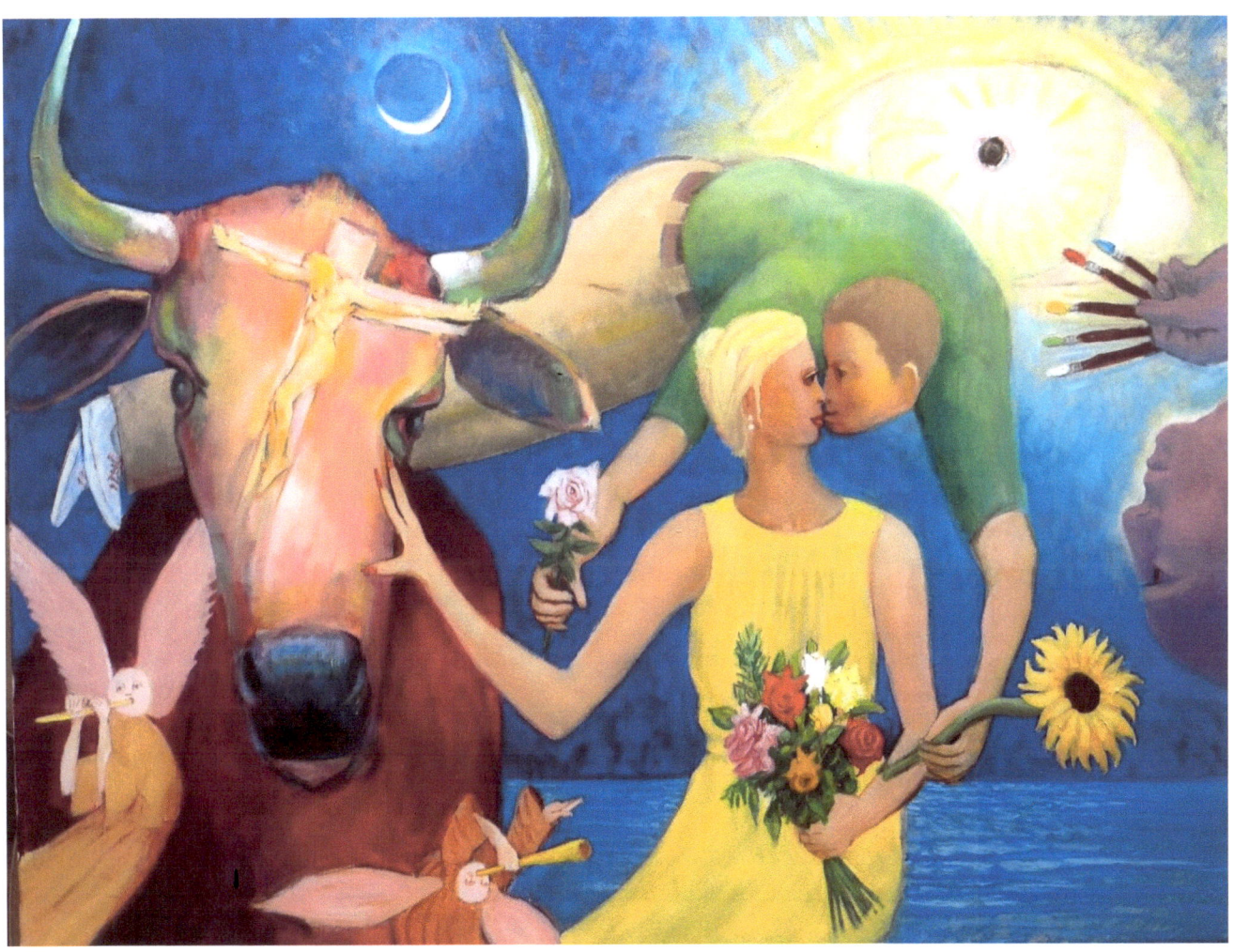

LETTING GO

(11x14 oil on canvas)

A young man, dressed for heavy weather, holds three white rabbits, indicators of prolific potential. It seems easier to hold onto things the way they are than to let go. Holding on to what is in hand, in the mind, in one's relationships seems safe, warm, comfortable, but it is very dangerous to what is being held as well as to the one holding tightly. Change always comes. Heavy weather is on the way, but not right now. The new, the evolved, will intrude into his life. But for now the sky is clear, a new day is dawning.

Preparation for the difficult and uncomfortable is important, but enjoying the momentary peace and comfort that blesses is also wise. Whether the environment is threatening or not, decisions must be made about what to hold closely. Being wise about what must be held as well as what must be free is very important. Eventually, the present form of everything, including relationships, must be let go of for it to become what it is evolving into. Holding anything too tightly for too long brings anger, resentment and deterioration. Eventually death will come from a strangle hold.

The number three usually suggests process or movement. All created things: animals, humans, even ideas and faith, must evolve. The young man understands this, but is reluctant to let go right now. He stands before the vastness of the ocean and is reminded how small he is, but he is not insignificant. He is vastly important to the Creator.

This is why an angel with pink wings descends to embrace the young man. The spiritual world supports him in his struggles. He will hold on until he feels it is right to let go. He has integrity. It will never be easy.

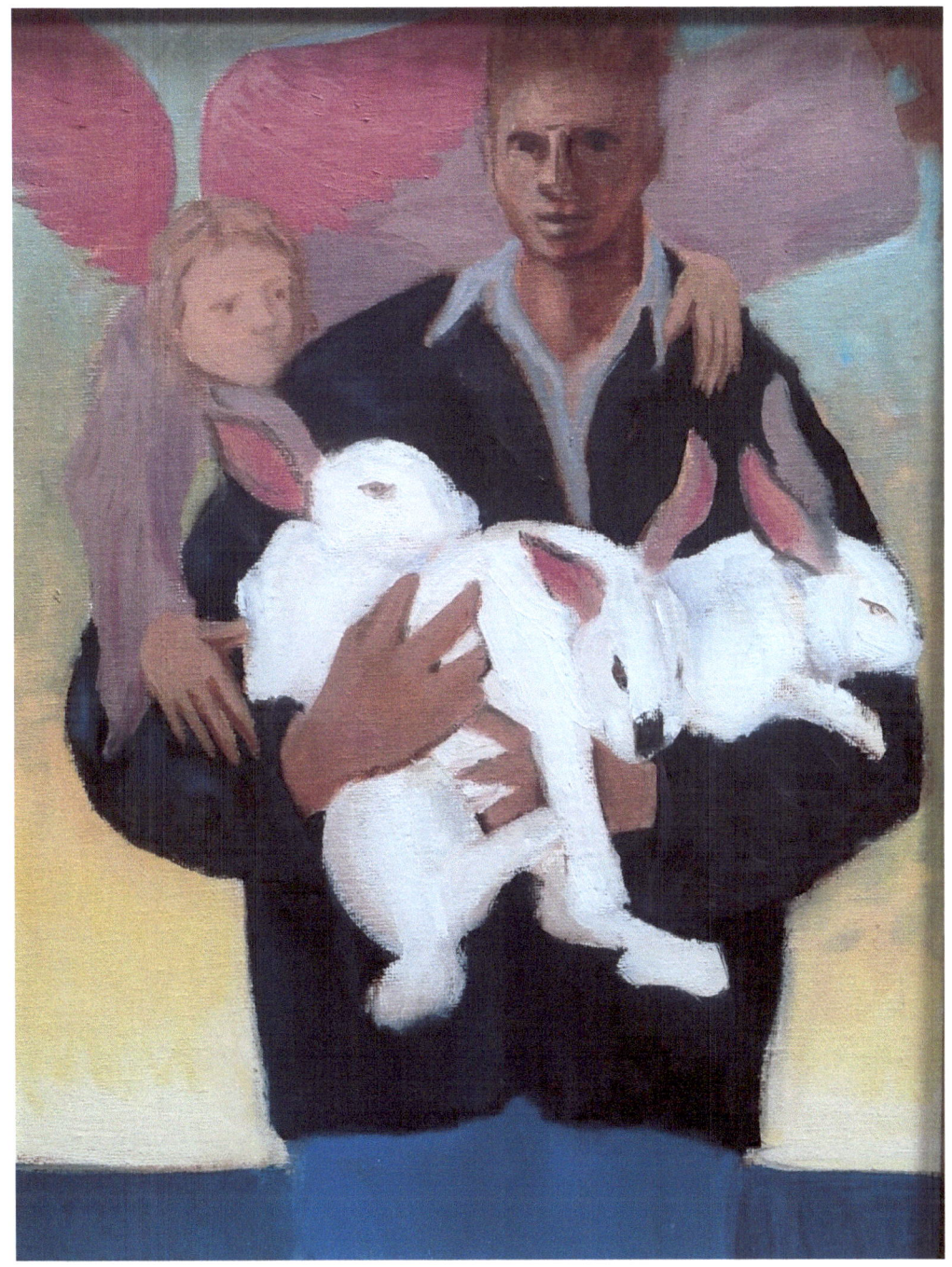

ANGEL AT THE GATE

(40x30 oil on canvas)

The angel is at the gate of Paradise lost. She stands resolutely as a warning and threat. The humans are in an instinctual, comfortable, and unconscious Paradise, as they taste the fruit of the Creator's wonderful garden. The taste is an awakening. The responsibility for deciding what is good and what is evil is now theirs. There is no going back. The gatekeeper swings a flaming sword in all directions. Their limited view of themselves and the world will fall to pieces. Trying to return to a former Eden cannot succeed.

Our primal parents and all succeeding Adams and Eves are tempted by an inner voice to partake of the Creator's supply of good fruit. It promises to make them wise. Adam and Eve do not realize they will die to their former unconscious comfort. They will be forced to see what they may not want to see, including their own mortality. Where instinct ruled in an Eden of dim awareness, now choices must be made between what can be evil or good in all the gifts of God's creation. Adam and Eve are attracted. Instinct empowers them. They consciously experience their sexuality. Expanded awareness calls for a new level of the knowledge of good and evil. It tempts them beyond their comfortable world and expels them into the knowledge of pain, guilt, and labor.

They cover their nakedness. The woman is beautiful and much to be desired. Her power to attract and to incubate life is irresistible. Their instinctual drives draw them into relationship. Their love is powerful. They are beginning to know the good and evil of it. No wonder there is a desire to return to a sleepy Paradise.

The serpent is part of God's created order. It is striped flesh-pink and vegetative-green and lives in any garden of partial truth. It tempts the humans toward further awareness. The rules of the present garden will have to be broken. Life sends the serpent-thought to whisper in Eve's and Adam's ears. Tasting more of life will always expel every Adam and Eve from their present Paradise. The man, Adam, is two-faced. With one face, he sees the desirable woman and all the fleshly joys and self-knowledge she represents. At the same time, he looks at the messenger of God guarding the gate and knows Paradise has been lost. The roots of the evergreen dig deep into the stardust of which all things are made.

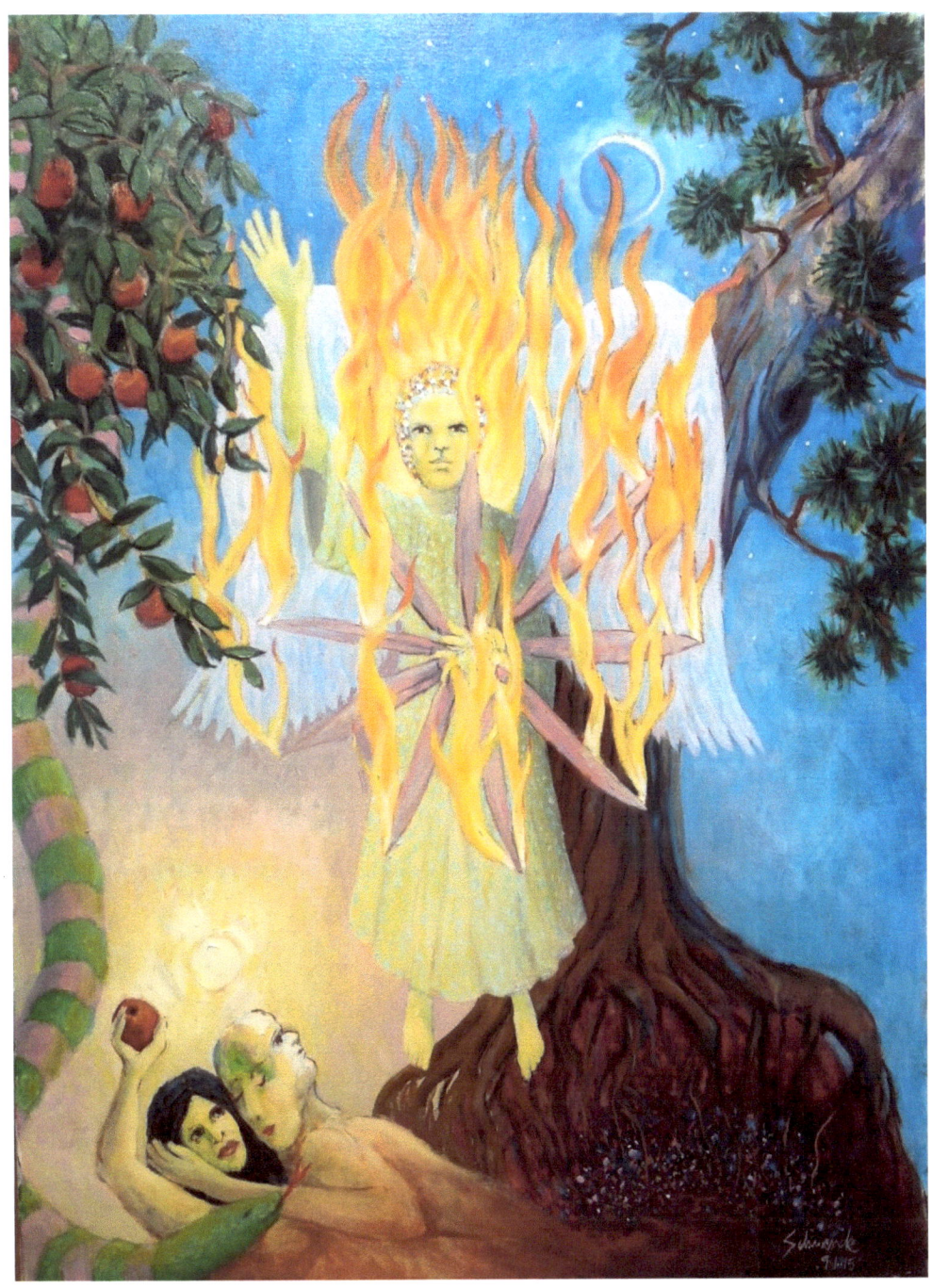

GRACE

(30x36 oil on canvas)

The sun blazes hot and spreads God's light on the elements of life. A sun-drenched angel holds a message for all to see: "Solo Gratia." Grace is faith, which comes as a pure gift. It's freedom that expands and creates. The awareness of this great gift comes through flesh, through human experience. The love of a mature couple is at the center. Their relationship is the channel of revelation. He releases the golden birds from the cage. One is reluctant to fly. Because he is free, others become free. Yet, he is quite conventional. The surface persona disguises the rebel. In her red dress, she tenderly supports his efforts. She is supported by an earthly and ethereal spirit with pink feminine wings.

The powerful beast climbs the insecure rope ladder, let down from heaven, reaching almost to earth. The beast, almost human, rises into the light. It has come from a dark place. The brute appears friendly and holds the artist's tools. The creative beast could be dangerous, but it is also a harlequin, a jokester intending no harm. It conveys a humbling truth about the conventional couple. The primitive power of the green brute and the stability of the conventional couple belong together, though there is tension.

The pastor stands on the sanctuary roof. He holds the signs of the costly communion offered by freeing grace: the wine and bread, the blood poured out, and body broken. The sacrament offered from the church is touched by a vague spirit from the earth. A riot of blossoms surrounds the places of worship, and the ancient bells ring out with invitation to worship the Creator.

The memorial arch blooms pink, while through it, the watcher observes the elements of faith. Death and loss heighten the value of life and its beauty. Behind the scene, the hand of God warns the beast not to go too high too quickly. Creativity must not get too distant from the earth and the fleshly experience of man and woman. The white-winged angel blows her horn, calling attention to the process which leads to faith and freedom. All is by Grace.

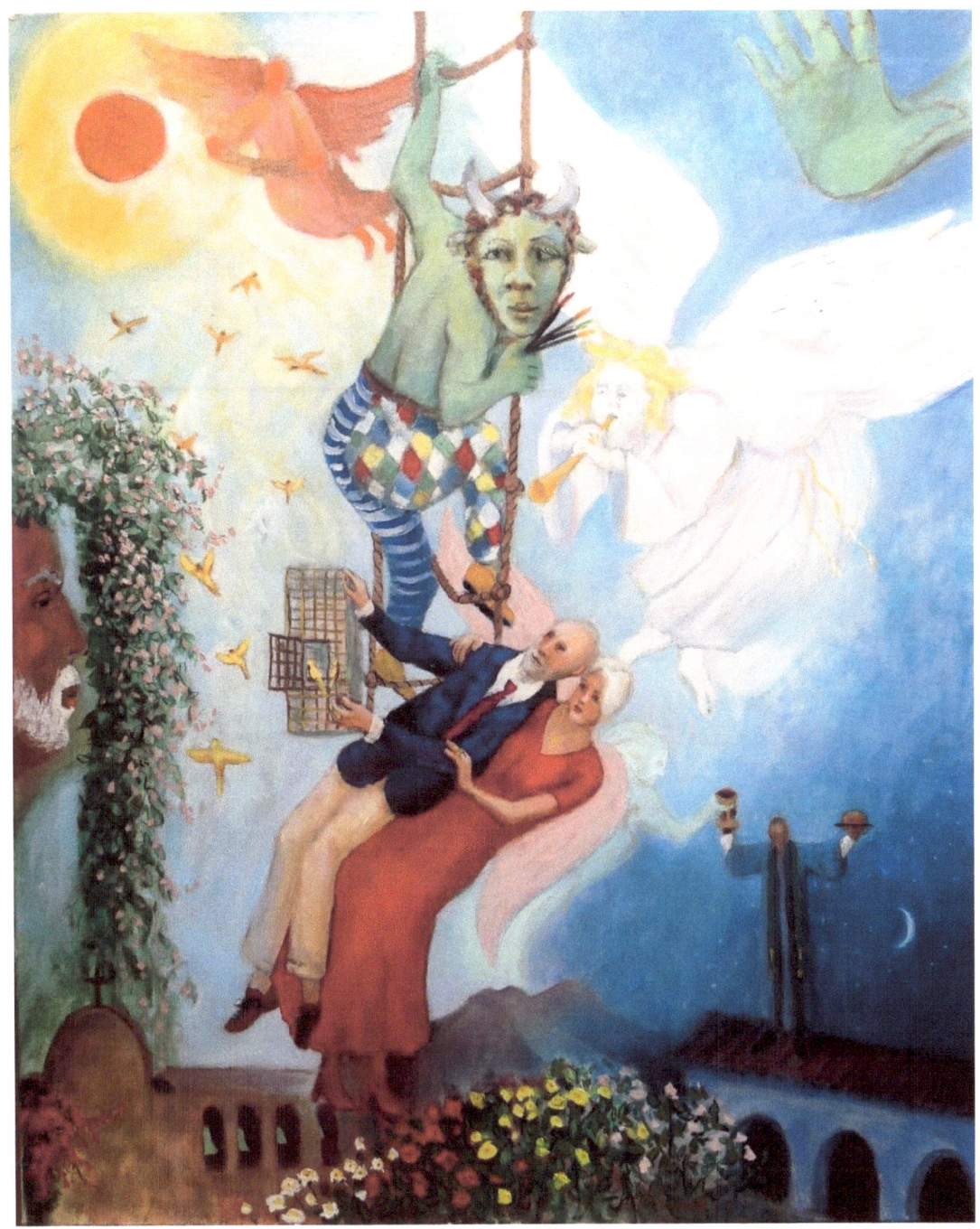

THE PRESENTION OF CHRIST

(40x30 oil on canvas)

The Great Red Winged Spirit descends from the hidden mysteries of heaven. The Spirit, iridescent and happy, presents the Christ, the cosmic "One is the All." The issue from and of the Father holds the fruit of Eden, the promise of the soul's growth and wholeness. In the garden, the knowledge of good and evil grows and tempts us out of our sleepy, instinct-driven comforts. To ingest the knowledge forbidden by the God of our comfortable immaturity, to take in this consciousness, is to begin to be whole. Soul food brings with it great responsibility. With eyes wide open, we see our pain, our inadequacies, and our failures, indicated by the nail marks in the Christ child's left hand. Yet it is our only path by which to grow into whole beings and mature souls. There are always wounds from this evolving individuation as well as eternity's blessings of hope and love.

A multitude of heavenly hosts sings, "Glory to God. Glory to God in the highest, and on earth, peace among men and women." Heaven and earth shout for joy and sing of the Creator's glorious grace. The angels flutter and swoop through the moonlit arch of pink roses, the memorial to a beloved daughter, taken too early from her sons. The flowering portal from earth to the heavenly realm and from the divine center to earthly, human experience is full of Creator's singing servants. They cluster around the presence of Christ everywhere and always.

The Spirit, with passionate wings, flies through the *ouroborous*, the tail-swallowing serpent. The beginning is the end, and the end is the beginning. It is full of human and divine elements, dynamically balanced and integrated. The moral Law of Moses, the great bull to be sacrificed, the feminine sensuality, the skull drained of life, the crucified Savior, the creative tools of the painter, the broken bread and poured-out wine of communion with this grace, the body and blood and spirit, are merging. The scripture, the Word, is within the starry sky, and the slice of moon is opposite the promise of morning. All is announced by the descending angel trumpeting Good News.

The cycle of life, prima material, is ready for the philosopher's stone and immortality of the soul. The faithful dog joyously sniffs out the path, which leads through the present activities, through the past experiences, and into the fullness and wholeness of God's kingdom. The canine spirit is beside us. The Christ Spirit is within our human experience. Flesh and blood are wounded, but by God's grace are destined for heaven. "Glory to God in the highest. Glory to God in the highest."

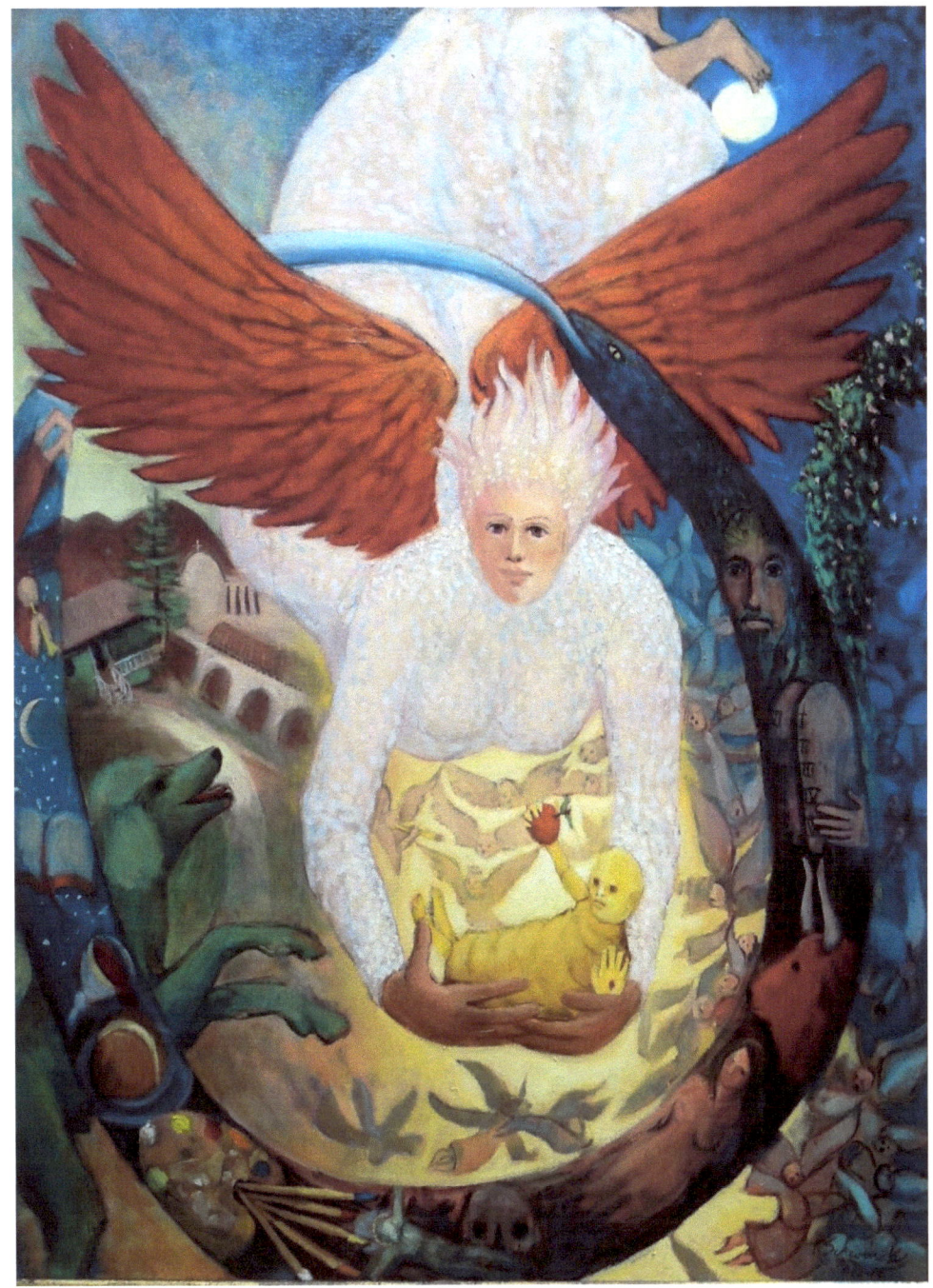

THE CENTER OF LIFE

(20x16 oil on canvas)

Christ is at the center of life. Like Father, like Son. The Creator's heart is revealed in the Son. Christ's wounds are a reflection of the suffering the Father willingly endures for the sake of relationship with his children. The Passion of Christ is the self-expression of our heavenly Father. His wounds are inflicted every day, every hour, ever moment, but still the Lord of heaven and earth comes to us. Even the angels of heaven are dumbfounded at such a sacrifice for the created. It is a holy surprise, a mysterious grace, a confusing commitment to comfort, to renew, to shepherd, to fulfill and to save.

The heavenly hosts sing, "Glory to God in the highest. Honor and majesty belong to him who gives himself for the sake of his creation."

The artist senses the spiritual presence behind the dazzling surface. All things are full of life and reflect the creative, sustaining, evolving power of their Maker. The artist seeks to bring this depth of life into focus on the canvas. As beautiful as the visible world is, it is only a dim hint of the brightness within. The creative one stands frustrated on a precarious perch to get a better view. It is shaky. He paints by the rose-covered arch, a memorial to a child gone, remembered, and grieved.

The façade and the bells of the ruined sanctuary still stand nearby. A riot of roses surrounds it, celebrating its past. From the earth, a spirit rises and gives praise of the Christ and also assists the artist. A lion peers out of the shadows below the living easel. It means to threaten. The trumpeting angel announces that the darkness has not overcome the light, though there are times of temporary eclipse.

The ministering Spirit dives down to caress the Christ in his weakness. Suffering and death will be overcome. Pain and loss will be removed, and the Christ will suffer no more when all brothers and sisters are whole. What has been hidden or only dimly perceived will fill all things with life eternal.

"Glory to God in the highest. Glory to God in the depths. Glory to God in the whole cosmos and in every spiritual place. Alleluia and Amen."

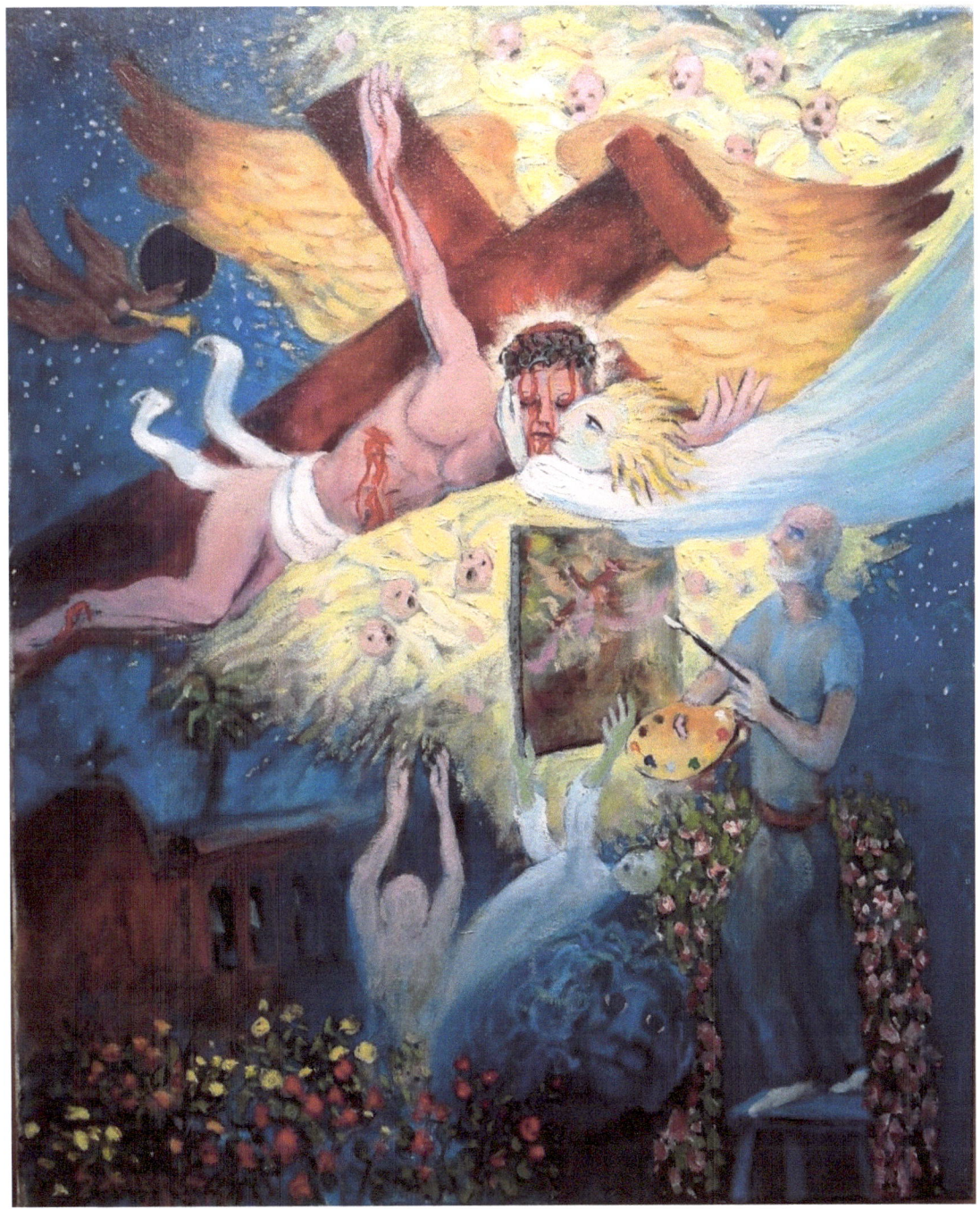

COMMUNION

(30x36 oil on canvas)

Communion is present in the middle of the Creator's beautiful bouquet of life. Each bloom of every sort is a gift, a good gift as it comes from the Creator's hand.

The pastor swoops down toward the communion table grasping the cup of blessing and the bread of life. Sacrifice of self-interest and even bodily life, seen in the passion of Christ, gives a glimpse of the Creator's commitment to be present in all life. The good from the hand of the Creator has not always remained good in the hand of God's children. Even in the midst of suffering, pain, and death, there is communion.

In times of darkness, as the flight of time hurries by, as death of loved ones brings us sorrow and grief, and as loss of significant work causes an identity crisis, communion exists. Life is short. Death intrudes. Personas evolve and fade. Still there is communion.

In times of sunshine and clarity of vision, there, too, is communion. In times of joyous bodily passion and the satisfying of sensual hungers, communion continues.

The Creator is with us always under every circumstance, in times of joy and times of grief, in times of successful work and of loss of opportunity, in times of vital bodily life and death, there communion is also.

Angels of all varieties declare it, celebrate it, inspire, and touch it. Human tradition, symbols, pious images, the sacred story, and sermon shout it out. Communion is eternal, under every circumstance, in every moment. Grace, mercy, love, truth, and joy are at the center of our lives.

Praise the God of Communion from whom all blessings flow.

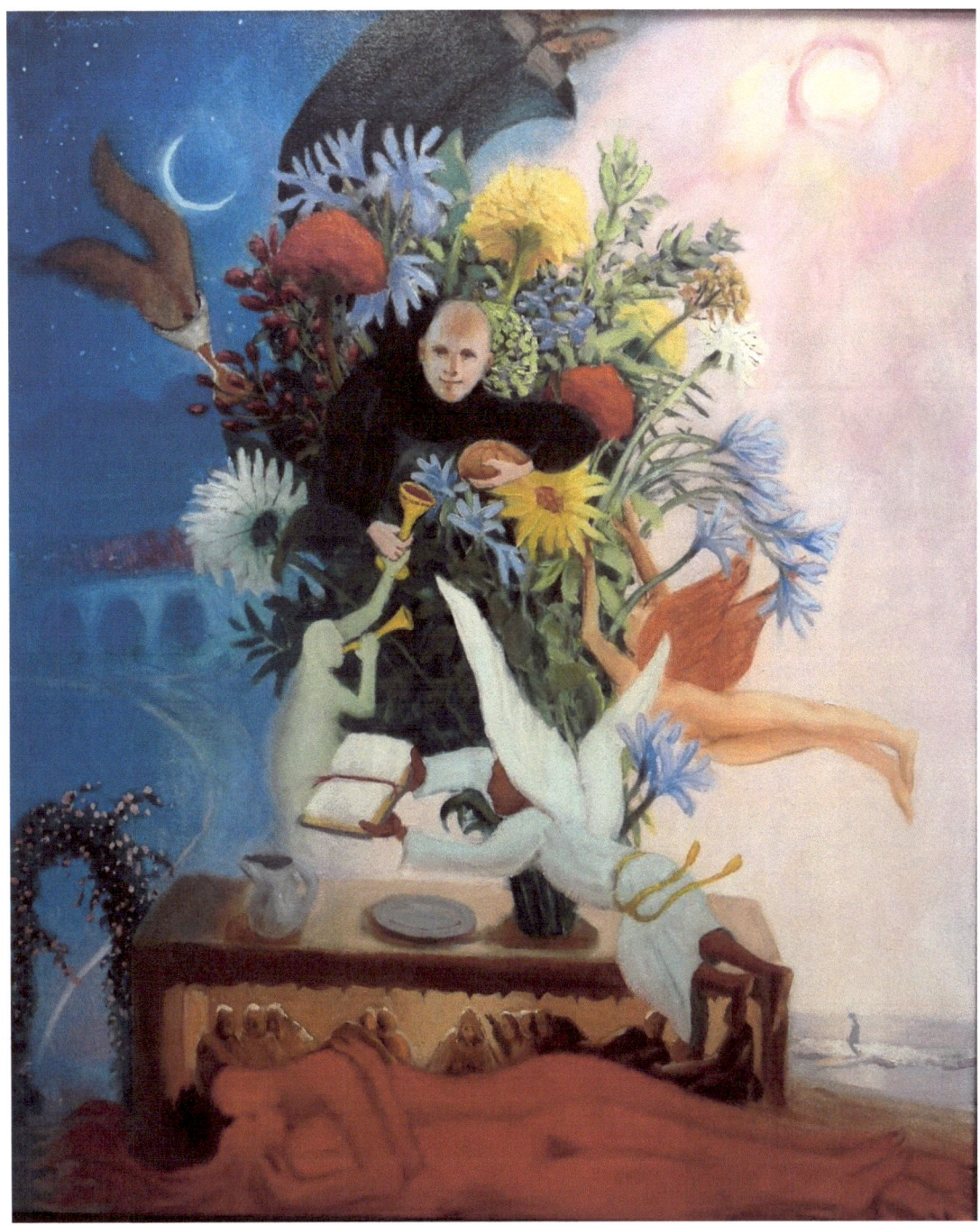

ABOUT THE AUTHOR

Robert L. Schwenck was born in Los Angeles and raised in Glendale, California. Living in a fair climate, surrounded by hills and near ocean, mountains, and desert inspired Bob at an early age to attempt to capture the beauty he observed around him. He received a National Art Association Scholarship and earned his Bachelor of Arts degree in Drawing and Painting from UCLA. But the ministry beckoned, and he went on to earn his Masters of Divinity from Princeton Seminary. During his thirty-seven years in the ministry (over thirty years serving the Community Presbyterian Church of San Juan Capistrano where he is now Pastor Emeritus), he continued to marvel at the beauty he saw in the world.

Bob Schwenck paints with clarity, strength and vitality. He uses saturated color and vigorous brushstrokes to communicate the creation's spiritual foundations.

In recent years he has had several one-man shows in Southern California including showing his work at Mission San Juan Capistrano and several private showings. He has done numerous commissions working both from photographs and on-the-spot drawings and has had his work displayed in local galleries in San Juan Capistrano and Dana Point. He is one of the featured artists in the book *Art of the American West* by Caroline Linscott and Julie Christiansen-Dull, a collection of the best work of contemporary western artists.

Robert L. Schwenck's work is displayed at The Cottage Gallery on Los Rios in San Juan Capistrano. Please stop by and see his paintings along with those of other exceptionally talented local artists.

He has served on the staff at Ghost Ranch in New Mexico teaching painting.

Robert Schwenck is an award-winning member of San Clemente Art Association and can be seen in shows throughout Southern California.

Now, happily retired, Bob Schwenck resides—and paints—in Dana Point, California with occasional trips to other locales in search of his next inspiration.

GLOSSARY OF IMAGES

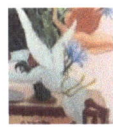 **Angels** - Servants of God who bring gifts and announce truth

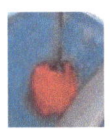 **Apple -** The fruit of Eden, disobedience that brings conscious and with it the awareness of human vulnerability, weakness, selfish passion , the passing of time and the reality of death

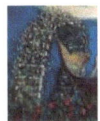 **Arch -** A memorial arch was erected for our daughter, Erin Lynne, who died August 25, 2010. It is flowering because she was a great blessing to us.

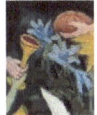 **Bread and Wine** - The Eucharist, communion elements, the body and blood of Christ, Crucifixion, food of grace, mercy and forgiveness resulting in the awareness of the presence of the Creator

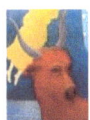 **Bull -** A powerful beast, an irresistible natural power that bring energy and danger to the temporary Eden of our self- view, the powerful energy of human creativity, which seems disruptive and dangerous

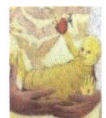 **Christ -** The child, God's gift of self within the human experience, the crucified, the love of the Creator encountering the evil of humans

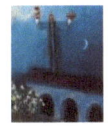 **Church -** My place of ministry for over 30 years

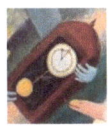 **Clock and Hourglass** - A vision of the gift of time and its short duration

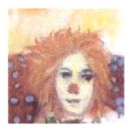 **Clown** - An activity loaded with eternal significance but becomes clownish in the hands of inadequate humans

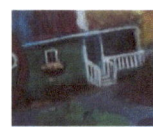 **Green House -** The Cottage Gallery where my landscapes are shown

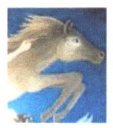 **Horse** - Literally horsepower—friendly, helpful, swift animal energy

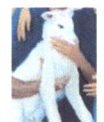 **Lamb** - The traditional symbol of innocence and specifically the purity of the Christ

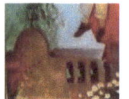 **Mission -** Historic Mission San Juan Capistrano

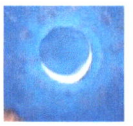 **Moon** - Reflected light in the unconscious, feminine and incubating energy, night is the time of dim consciousness

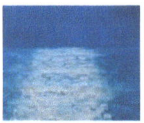 **Ocean -** Reminder of the vastness of the physical universe, the depths of the unknown from which all creativity flows

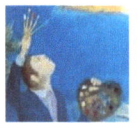 **Palette and Brushes** - Tools of the artist, a gift and a means of revelation

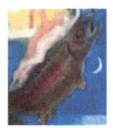 **Rainbow Trout -** A multifaceted presence that dwells in the depths; occasionally it leaps into consciousness but falls back into dim unconsciousness quickly

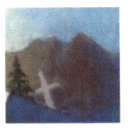 **Saddleback Mountain -** The major geological element in the Capistrano Valley reminds us of our attachment to the earth, how we are made from dust

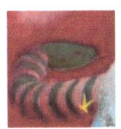 **Serpent** - The voice of human development that comes from our inner landscapes and seeks spiritual growth and expanded awareness

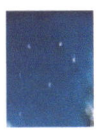 **Stars** - Indicating the vastness of the cosmos and hinting of eternity

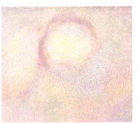 **Sunligh**t - The time of clarity and awareness, consciousness

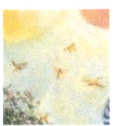 **Swallows** - Usually there are seven, referring to the spirits of our seven grandchildren

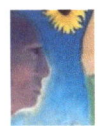 **Watcher** - At times all we can do is stand on the sidelines a watch unable to do anything other than become aware that our lives are evolving and expanding

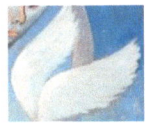 **Wings** - A sign of spiritual presence

www.ingramcontent.com/pod-product-compliance
Lightning Source LLC
Chambersburg PA
CBHW050757180526
45159CB00003B/1497